Nature Safari

Geoff Sample

Collins is an imprint of
HarperCollinsPublishers Ltd.
77–85 Fulham Palace Road
London
W6 8JB

The Collins website address is:
www.collins.co.uk

First published in 2003
08 07 06 05 04 03

10 9 8 7 6 5 4 3 2 1

ISBN 0-00-713839-3

The copyright in the images belongs to Geoff Sample apart from the following:
Sharon Bailey p.80 (top); p115 (bottom); p.122; p146 (top); Cabarrus County p.184;
Collins p.29 (below); p.172; p.178; Embraer Aircraft Company: p.15; NASA: p.162;
p.170 (below right); p.176; p.177; Nature Photographers Ltd: p.1; p.14; p.18 (below);
p.25; p.26; p.30; p.31; p.32; p.34 (below); p.36; p.37; p.38; p.39; p44; p.46 (top left);
p.48; p.49; p.52; p.56 (top); p.59 (top and centre); p.62 (top); p.64; p.69; p.70; p.71;
p.72; p.73; p.74; p.75; p.76; p.77; p.78; p.84 (top); p.85 (top); p.86; p.87; p.91; p.93;
p.94; p.101 (left); p.105; p.109 (below); p.111; p.112; p.114; p.115 (top); p.117; p.118;
p.120; p.121; p.123; p.124; p.126; p.127; p.133; p.136; p.137 (below); p.140; p. 141;
p.142; p.148; p.150 (top); p.151; p.153; p.154; p.155; p.156; p.157; p.158; p.160; p.164;
p.167 (top); p.170 (top); p.175; p.181; p.182; Ordnance Survey: p.22 (below); p.161;
Ian Patience: p.9; p.16; p.30; p60; p.65 (top); p.102; p.113; p.130; p.171;
Virigina Living Museum p.185

Colour reproduction by Colourscan, Singapore
Printed and bound in Singapore by Imago

Contents

Introduction

Welcome. You stand at the doorway about to enter a maze of paths that all lead to different discoveries and further doorways, but are connected by one thread: nature – the system of life that has evolved on the earth. An understanding of nature is useful in so much of our lives – particularly when it comes to maintaining a good living environment for ourselves; but an enjoyment of the world of nature is a gift that becomes more and more valued as you grow older.

This book is for those of you who like spending time outdoors and want to know and see more in the natural world. It is not an identification guide, though it should provide you with a good basis for moving on to identifying species. If you find you have a growing interest for one particular area, then you should think about getting a more specific guide. Collins publishes a variety of good identification guides for both beginners and specialists.

Read on to find explanations, suggestions, ideas and practical tips to help you get more out of your time in the countryside, town parks and gardens: dip in and follow the threads that lead you into this strange and beautiful world that we live in – planet earth.

Our region of the world, the northern half of Europe, is a densely-populated area, apart from the far north, where the long, cold winters make life hard for man and beast. As well as large built-up areas in and around cities, much of the countryside gets used for agriculture, forestry, mineral extraction, leisure, sport and many other activities that affect the nature of a place and its wildlife. In intensively farmed fields there is not much scope for wildlife (plants, insects or other animals) to survive.

Nevertheless there are very few places that have no wildlife interest at all. Nature is a dynamic force that is constantly renewing itself, seeking to spread out and diversify. Any neglected ground is soon invaded by nature's front line: first come the weeds, scorned by gardeners, but actually very successful opportunist plants, whose seeds travel well – and often have very pretty flowers. As the ground vegetation increases, in come insects and small rodents, then their predators. In fact, waste ground in cities can be a haven for wildlife and often becomes a temporary Nature Reserve.

Nature safari

Take a look down at the tracks if you travel on the London underground; mice live down there. Birds get everywhere, even to the heart of cities. Foxes are now more common in many English towns and cities than in the countryside. Most towns and cities have parks with a pond or lake and some have canals or rivers running through them providing an opportunity to see some aquatic life.

If you don't look, you don't see. Or as the song goes: 'Fishing for a good time starts with throwing in your line'. So go on, throw in your line.

Some of the ideas in the book are quite complex and take some time to understand: but that's the way it is in exploring nature – take your time. The words written in italics are defined in the glossary at the end of the book. There are also links to related subjects provided at the bottom of the pages.

▲ Look for dragonflies around woodland pools on sunny summer days.

The door to nature

Nature in legend and history

In the modern world our lives are so wrapped up with the products of our technologies that it is easy to forget about that other world surrounding us — the natural world, where things go on much as they have done for millions of years.

There's a timelessness in nature: we can find clues to the past and feel a real sense of ages past. As you stand in a tall forest you are within something that spans a greater breadth of time than human memory. Previous generations may have stood in this same place centuries ago and watched the same sky and the same birds, heard the same wind rustling the leaves and felt the same cool shade.

And yet scientists and philosophers are still seeking to understand the basic questions about nature. Why does this happen? What substances does this contain? How did life begin? Where did the world come from?

Human beings have been examining the natural world and asking these same questions for many thousands of years — in fact, ever since we developed the power to think of something more than where to get our next meal. As you can imagine, explanations for things have changed much over the years.

▲ Bison painted on a cave wall many thousands of years ago.

Caves are mysterious places: they are dark, with hidden corners, a creepy dampness and always the possibility of a secret history. After all, not so long ago, we used caves for shelter. Well maybe not *we,* but our ancestors. They were also the scenes of our ceremonies and their associated art.

On September 12th 1940, four teenagers were exploring some woods in southern France, when they came across a hole in the ground where a

▲ A hunting scene.

large pine tree had fallen. The opening led into a cave and, peering into the dim light of its hidden corners, they could just make out some fantastic paintings of animals and hunting scenes on the walls. Something about the scenes suggested the paintings were ancient and experts later dated them to 17,000 years ago. Nearby there are other caves with 30,000 year-old paintings. Now that's old art.

The people who made these paintings were fascinated by the animals around them; and in days before farming, when hunting for meat and gathering fruits and berries were so much more important, a good understanding of the natural world was THE KNOWLEDGE for sheer survival. So, it's maybe not so surprising that these paintings, the earliest human art, were of the wild animals they hunted, and on whom they depended.

Some historians think the pictures were used in teaching the young members of the tribe about hunting techniques (imagine a painted cave for your classroom!). Others think the pictures were part of magic or religious ceremonies that took place in the caves.

Nature Safari

project

do your own prehistoric cave painting

Try to find a book in your library that has some pictures of real cave paintings and take a close look at how the animals have been drawn and painted. Yes, they're quite well designed, considering they were produced by cavemen!

Pick your favourite animal and try to draw/paint it just as if it were a cave painting. Use simple lines that show the character of the animal. OK, you can do a dinosaur if you want. You could try it on paper first. Mark in some outlines lightly with a pencil for a guide, then try it in colour with crayons or paint. Reds and blacks were the main colours used by the cavemen (you could try to find out why).

Then, if you have a rock with a suitable surface – best check with your parents first – you could maybe try it for real. You might have to experiment on a smaller rock to find which crayons or paints give the best results.

Legends

So cast your mind back to those earlier times. Yes, way before television. No shops either. Nor much in the way of houses, just caves and make-shift shelters. How might you spend the evening after a hard day's hunt? Telling stories, of course. About great hunts and hunters, encounters with strange beasts, and suchlike. And remember there were no books for you to check the facts about an animal: you had to rely on your own experience and the stories of the older people in your family or tribe.

There would also have been stories about where the world came from, who was the first man, what happens when someone dies. Then there may have been a little dance around a fire, imitating the motions of some of the more impressive creatures in your world, with some singing or simple music.

Early stories are full of tales involving animals and their ways. Ravens for instance crop up in different stories from throughout Europe. Sometimes they foretell death – well, they are large and black and eat dead animals; sometimes it's their cunning that is the main theme.

Mythical beasts

Most countries of the world have their stories of mythical beasts, monsters of various shapes: griffins, unicorns, yetis, giant bears, Cyclops and other creatures that dwell in the caverns of the mind. Water monsters seem to be common in northern Europe. Scotland's Loch Ness monster is a well-known example. Could a relic of the dinosaur age be living in the depths of a large mountain lake? What does it eat? Or is it a seal of mistaken identity? Or a figment of the imagination, when the light dances across the surface ripples? No one can say for sure.

Ravens

The Viking god of wisdom and war, Odin, was said to have strange, supernatural powers. He had two ravens who spent the night on his shoulders: their names were Mind and Memory. Each morning he would send them out into the world and in the evening when they returned they would perch on his shoulders and tell him of what they had seen going on in the world – one in each ear. Today we have news reporters on the television to tell us what is going on.

Think about this: why, in old stories, are there so many birds and animals that can talk? And in modern cartoons? Even our scientific world has traces of ancient legends still alive. For centuries there have been ravens living around the Tower of London. It has always been said that when the ravens leave the Tower, England will be no more. Nowadays the flight feathers of their wings are clipped by the raven keeper. So there is little chance of them flying off!

Plant legends

There is much in legend about the power of plants for healing illnesses and casting spells. Whereas some of these are based on superstitions about warding off evil spirits, many have been found to work and have a scientific explanation. Garlic, for instance, is said to be effective at keeping off vampires; fortunately I have never had to deal with a vampire. However, it might be more useful to know that garlic is believed to be good for stopping cuts becoming infected and, when eaten, for preventing coughs and colds.

▼ Ramsons or wild garlic flowering in May

Different extracts from roses are thought to be good for headaches and sore throats. The next time you get a nettle sting, try a dock leaf. I was told to spit on the leaf, then rub it gently on the stings. It seems to work, though I've yet to read any explanation for it. Try it.

Secrets of the past

There are many mysterious signs of our prehistoric ancestors scattered around the landscape: rings of standing stones, like the magnificent Stonehenge, long barrows, cairns, earthworks, rocks carved with ring and cup patterns, and burial chambers. 'Prehistoric' means before written history, so all we can tell about these peoples is what we can discover from such remains. This is the work of archaeologists.

Story-telling has always been an important part of our love of nature. Knowledge is passed on from generation to generation by the telling of encounters with strange animals or mysterious places, often exaggerated with a little imagination to make more of a story. There's a saying: 'It gets bigger in the telling'.

Links

finding
prehistoric sites
p.22

▲ The carved shapes on this rock were made around 4,000 years ago: there are similar patterns in many places in the world. No one knows for sure what they mean.

Nature Safari

Investigation – science

You may have heard humans referred to as 'Homo sapiens': scientists use this phrase to define our species as modern humans. It means 'wise human', as opposed to 'Homo habilis' (domestic human) who we are descended from. Philosophers decided that the real distinguishing characteristic of humans, the thing that makes us different from our ancestors, is our intelligence. I know sometimes this can be difficult to believe!

The myths and legends of different peoples make up mankind's early attempts to explain what they saw in the world around them. Sometimes there were rather strange explanations.

The strange case of the barnacle goose and the goose barnacle

Barnacle geese spend much of the cooler part of the year on the shores of northern Europe; but between spring and late summer they disappear, then return again in the autumn. Now this puzzled people.

▼ A goose barnacle colony washed up on the shore.

But in these regions a certain shellfish grows into rich colonies on tree logs washed into the sea. They hang from the wood by a rubbery neck-like extension and look quite like goose heads. It was said until quite recently that these were young barnacle geese, thinking that barnacle geese did not hatch from normal eggs like other birds, but grew from these shellfish; so they became known as goose barnacles. Once the breeding grounds of barnacle geese were discovered, high up in the Arctic, the geese were found to have the same origins as any other birds – from an egg laid by a mother goose.

▲ Barnacle goose: spends the summer in the high Arctic.

Gradually science has revealed a clearer picture of our natural world and often contradicted the old stories; but these stories show how our ancestors felt about the world around them, how their minds worked and many old stories have an element of truth in them. Scientists try to find the true explanations for how and why things happen.

In science it is particularly useful if you can test an explanation. In the case of the barnacle geese, we could use modern methods to track the geese to their breeding grounds and map out where they spend the summer; or we could develop a colony of goose barnacles to maturity in a laboratory and describe the results.

An unusual thing about science is that the result is often less important than the method. You may prove or disprove a theory, but either way the notes and measurements made during an experiment are important information for anyone else investigating the same subject. It is the same with observing nature: you can watch things for fun, try an experiment to learn a little more, but the really sharp nature detective keeps notes.

These are the main areas of studying the nature of the world:

Geology: *the study of the rocks and minerals that make up the earth*
Biology: *the study of how living things work*
Zoology: *the study of different plants and animals*
Ecology: *the study of the connections between animals, plants and their environments*

project

why do aeroplanes and birds have similar wings?

There are always things to discover in the wild world, and not just new species or new substances; many inventors have found their original ideas by observing how things work in nature.

To find the answer to this question, you should begin by discovering how people have tried to fly in the past; and how was the first aeroplane invented. A good start would be to find out about Leonardo da Vinci. You could also look up the legend of Icarus. Try an encyclopaedia or the internet: do a search on 'flight' and 'wing'.

Embraer aircraft company

project

keep a diary

Who knows, one day you may become a famous *ecologist* or snake expert, and your first diaries may be valuable collector's items. They could be just written notes of what you see on walks in your street or in your garden; you could make regular observations at the same place each day or at a certain time of day. Make a note of the date, what the weather is like, where you visit, what you see and what it is doing.

Or you could be a bit more artistic and include some illustrations, if you enjoy drawing and painting. It is best if you base your pictures on the real world rather than copy other illustrations, since you will see and learn more about nature and your diary will be so much more interesting and valuable to other naturalists. Expert bird-watchers always keep notes on what they see and the best ones also include sketches showing details of interest.

One of the main ways into nature is through the seasons. You become aware of the details of the seasonal changes in the world around you. Summer may be a comfortable time to be out and about, but there is something of interest at all times of the year – though not always in the same place through each season.

Changing seasons

In the northern half of Europe people have always eagerly looked for signs of spring – signs that the cold months were coming to an end and new life returning. Snowdrops are an early hint that winter will not go on for ever, but primroses have always been taken as a sign that spring has begun.

▲ Primroses in flower.

Groups of neat yellow flowers with deep green leaves make primroses easily recognised. They are a fairly common plant of light woods, clearings and hedgerows, that flower early, before the grass has grown to overshadow them. You sometimes find them in meadows, well away from the nearest trees. This is usually a sign that the place was woodland not too long ago. The first flowers can appear any time from February in a mild year in the south to April in the north.

Another sign of spring coming is the catkins on 'pussy willow'. These are actually the tree's flowers and usually appear around February.

◄ Pussy willow – an early sign of spring.

An obvious sign of the changing seasons is the dying leaves falling from trees in the autumn. Different kinds of trees vary in how long they can hang on to their leaves. Oaks do very well. You could make a note of the date when your nearest oak tree becomes bare each year. It varies depending on when the first frosts arrive and how much the autumn gales blow.

▲ Sycamore leaf dying in the autumn.

Other events that mark the changing seasons:

First swallow to return in spring; the last to go in autumn.
First cuckoo heard in spring
First frog spawn seen in the early spring
Ripening corn in summer
The first frost of autumn
The first snow of winter

Now, if you really want to give your diary an edge, you might think of adding some weather data in your notes. Yes, 'data': you're now giving your diary a scientific basis. A simple way to do this is to hang a *thermometer* outside, so you can tell the temperature. Your seasonal observations will now be tied in with measurements of weather conditions.

Links

weather and seasons p.163

Nature Safari

Space for the imagination

Every kind of animal and plant has its own preferences for the sort of place it can live and this is called its *habitat*. But the typical places we humans are drawn to are often a mix of habitats. Some places, whether sheltered and cosy or maybe open and spectacular, are simply nice places to spend time, explore what is there or play games. It could be a riverside meadow or a moorland valley with a tree-lined river. Good spots often become picnic sites, parks or possibly local nature reserves. They may have a strong atmosphere or character to them. Such places can make great spots for games of the imagination.

Natural sites are great for acting out scenes from the past, from books or films. It is easy to see a place as it was in past times – maybe not too different from how it is now. Or you can push it a little further on in time – somewhere on a distant planet or a future world. Take a look around and see what the character of the place is, what might have happened here; what does it remind you of, where else could you be in the world, in the universe, or even in time?

Places with a strong character or atmosphere have often been thought of as sites of power. The kind of place where a wizard would choose to meet his enemies or where you might find a door to another world. Is it only in the imagination? You will never know without looking.

▼ A mushroom-shaped water tower on the horizon? In our family it has always been 'the alien spaceship'.

Special places

▲ St Cuthbert's Cave – anyone for a game of hide-and-seek?

In the woods

Woodland clearings are nice places to spend time in any season. They provide a pitch, an arena for action. Hide-and-seek is a great game for a woodland clearing, especially if there is something you can use as base in the centre of the clearing. Surrounding bushes and trees should provide plenty of hiding places; the seeker will be drawn out from base to look into the bushes and this gives hiders a chance to make a sudden run for base. And you may just find a robin arrive on a branch to take a look at you as you are hiding in its territory.

The trunks of fallen trees make good seats with a backrest provided by the up-turned roots or branches. If there's a hidden spot, maybe behind a few boulders, this would make a good base for a team. Don't climb on trees or rocks when it is wet though, in case you slip or fall.

Bird's eye view

Many of the larger birds that soar in the air are fond of sitting at a high perch where they can get a good look out. This has inspired people to think of a high view in terms of what a bird, with its mastery of the air, might see. The look-out seat at the top of the masts of old sailing ships was known as the crow's nest; from here, whoever was on duty, would scan the distant horizon for other ships, land, whales and storms.

▼ Almost touching the clouds.

Of course, now we can rise high in the air, travelling on aeroplanes or balloons; so the ability to see like a bird is no longer so inaccessible. It is not always convenient (or cheap!) to take a flight on a plane, but you can always climb up to a good view point to get something of the same feeling. You can try somewhere with a view for miles, picking out distant landmarks in a wide horizon; or a spot up a hillside overlooking a valley, where you can watch the comings and goings of humans as well as any wildlife.

On top of the world

Old castles and forts were often built at sites which are good view points, the sort of place where you might see a marauding band of attackers several miles away as they approached; where your enemies would have to struggle up hill to attack your settlement, while you have the advantage of height; where summer breezes keep the biting flies down in the swampy forests below (there was much more marshland and forest in past times).

Where would you build a fort to guard this sea inlet? Is that an old fort there? Many species of bird also find security in a place with a good lookout. Eagles like to roost and nest on a ledge of a high crag, where they can see all around them. No, not through the rock behind them! They don't need to, because the rock itself provides protection and shelter. An eagle's nest site is called its eyrie (pronounced 'eye-ree'). These magnificent hunters need large territories and some of the best eyries have been in use for centuries by generation after generation of eagles.

▼ Bamburgh castle – built to guard the coast.

Carved in rock

▲ The Caves of Kilhern: an ancient burial chamber.

▼ Can you find the Caves of Kilhern on the map?

In many areas of northern Europe thick ice sheets covered the earth for a long period up to 10,000 years ago. They scraped the land back to rock and gravel; and in hilly and mountainous areas *glaciers* carved out deep valleys. From a good look-out point try to imagine the landscape stripped of vegetation and see if you can recognise any effects of the ice-age.

A thought to keep you going: however hard a slog it is getting up a hill, it is much easier when you're coming down.

project

find an Iron-age or Roman fort

2,000 years ago it was a time of changes throughout Europe. Celtic tribes were wandering westwards looking for new lands to settle in (which they often had to fight for). Then the Roman armies pushed north from Italy forcing the Celts and other peoples to recognise the laws of Rome. In Britain they never quite managed to deal with the wild country and its peoples in the north, the area of modern Scotland, and the Emperor Hadrian built a large wall in Northumberland to mark and defend Roman territory.

So these were unsettled times, when it was important to have a safe place for times of attack and somewhere that was easy to defend. This was a period when hill forts were useful, as they offered a good lookout over the surrounding forest.

Get a detailed map of your area (such as Ordnance Survey map with a scale of 1:50,000). Look down the side for the key or legend to find what the right symbols are for archaeological and historic information. Starting from where you live, examine the map to find the nearest historic symbols. It might be easier to use a magnifying glass and draw larger versions of the symbols shapes on a piece of note-paper.

See if you can find the symbol for an old fort, battlefield or burial site on the map. Find out who built it and when. How did they live and what was the land like? If you can't find anything on the map ask one of your parents or a teacher for some help.

Then visit it. Persuade one of your parents to take you there. It might not be easy, since you may find that the real place is not what you expected from the map. It may have changed. There may be a new road or a wood may have been felled. And there may be very little sign left of any building – maybe just a slight mound.

When you are there, you could try to picture in your mind what the place was like in previous times and describe it. If you had been born in a family there years ago, how would you have lived? If you enjoy drawing or painting, you could do two pictures showing the place now and how you think it may have looked when it was being used.

Ways of life – survival

Where we live

Often when we talk about the 'home' of an animal or plant, we actually mean the particular kind of *environment* it prefers – in other words – its *habitat*. There are some species that can find a home in a whole range of habitats; wrens, for instance, can be found in town gardens, marshes and even high moors. But many animals need very particular conditions.

Animals often live in different ways at different stages of their lives. In insects and amphibians this is quite extreme and they undergo a *metamorphosis*, where their body changes between different stages: from tadpole to adult frog, from hungry underwater larva to adult free-flying dragonfly, from caterpillar to chrysalis (pupa) to butterfly. At each stage their bodies are adapted to living a certain kind of life.

▼ Crabs have a skin-like armour.

Our homes

Until people learned how to farm the land – growing crops and herding animals, our ancestors had to move around in search of food. They made their homes in caves and temporary shelters, since it would not have been worth the effort of building permanent ones. They hunted wild animals for meat, using bones for tools and furs for clothes, and gathered *edible* plants, nuts, berries, mushrooms and suchlike. Humans living in this way are called 'hunter-gatherers' and maybe we still have those *instincts* within us.

When farming was developed, it made more sense to stay in one place to look after the animals and crops. At about the same time, people were also learning how to use metals like bronze and iron. Metal tools were tougher and, along with increasing skills in shaping rock and stone, helped us to build stronger houses and, with fire, clear some of the forests. Settlements became more permanent.

Animals' homes

Not many animals have a home in the sense of a house: rabbits, badgers, foxes and some other, usually small, mammals have dens – maybe a hole dug in the ground or a crevice in some rocks. Most animals tend to wander around their areas, but often have regular places for resting where they feel safe.

▼ Song thrush and family in the nest.

Links

mammals p.46, tracks and signs p.148

Birds build nests of sticks and straw, in which to lay their eggs and rear young, but outside the breeding season it is unusual for a bird to use a nest. Some types of bird may have regular perches which they use for spying or regular sites for roosting at night; but other species wander more widely. Swifts are thought to spend their whole lives in flight other than when they come in to their nests. You can often tell where a bird regularly roosts for the night by the pile of white droppings on the ground below.

Fish are rather like birds in this respect: some have cracks in the rocks which they use rather like dens, or favourite runs in a stream in which they like to lie (they are still swimming, but fishermen say they 'lie'). Many kinds of fish are constantly on the move, even if there is some pattern to the routes they take.

Nature safari

Shells

The outer bodies of many insects and *crustaceans* (crabs and lobsters) is a tough casing with joints so that the animals can move their limbs. The shells of tortoises and snails are hard and stiff, so the softer parts of their bodies come out of the shell to enable them to move. When danger threatens they withdraw quickly back into their shells. The extra weight of the shell means all these animals move slowly.

▲ A wild tortoise in Greece.

▶ 'Robin's pin cushion' – actually a wiry growth produced by the rose in which a small gall wasp larva lives.

Next time you are on the beach, look for a dead crab (check that it's not too smelly!) or a crab's leg or pincers and you'll see how they only move at the joints. What does it remind you of ? Maybe the arms of a crane or a digger? Crab's legs only move back and forth in one direction, which is why a crab runs sideways.

The strange case of the caddis fly larva

Snails, tortoises and turtles are the nearest examples in nature to an animal that carries a house around with it. But there are some creatures that actually build a shell-like house around themselves. The next time you're by a stream in summer, take a close look in the waters edge or under some stones. You might see some small tubes of gravel moving around. Inside this is the caterpillar-like larva of a caddis fly. It builds a case around itself then sticks gravel and bits of twig from the stream bed onto the case. Good camouflage and protection.

▼ The case of a caddis fly larva.

Hermit crab

Hermit crabs have a two-way protection. The back part of the bodies of these crabs is soft and vulnerable; so they use empty snail shells as their 'home'. Their head, legs and claws, on the front of their bodies, are as tough as any other kind of crab. As they grow, they leave one shell behind and use another slightly larger one. But it is quite a weight to drag around with them.

▼ Hermit crabs move into empty shells.

Finding food

All animals must eat something to provide them with energy for living. And over the billions of years that life has been evolving, different creatures have become adapted to feed in different ways. Some animals eat vegetable matter, whereas others eat meat; but all animals eat *organic* stuff – living material. Only plants can live off basic chemical *nutrients* (along with water and sunlight).

▲ Buzzard – birds of prey have hooked beaks for tearing off pieces of food.

Whereas some animals can eat a wide range of foods, many species have become specialised to take particular foods. Wading birds usually have long legs for paddling in the edge of pools and long beaks for probing into mud and sand for worms and suchlike. Butterflies and moths have long tubes for mouths through which they can suck up the sugar juices at the heart of flowers.

Without plant material there would be no food for any animals, even the meat-eaters. How is that? Well, let's take a look at life in a large pond or lake and work our way back.

▲ Curlews have long, probing beaks for finding worms in the mud.

Food chains

You may think that the shark-like pike is the ultimate *predator*; well that's almost true of the creatures living under the water surface, but even pike provide a meal for various creatures that live on land and do a little fishing. Humans, otters, ospreys (large fish-eating hawks) and bears will all make a meal of a pike when they get the chance. This makes them the top predators, though the pike is the top predator in its *aquatic* world.

Pike feed mostly on smaller fish and sometimes frogs and young waterbirds; the smaller fish, frogs and waterbirds feed mostly on insects, worms and suchlike. Some of those insects may be predators in their own right feeding on other insects or even tadpoles. But supporting all these predators are those creatures that eat vegetable matter – the grazers, such as tadpoles, various insects and their larvae, worms and pond-snails. Some of these eat the leaves of growing plants while others eat the small bits and pieces of decaying leaves and animal bodies.

And this is what we call a food chain: from the plant leaf to the top predator, it is all inter-linked. If one of the links disappears, then there is no food for the creatures further up the chain. Let's say for instance that a chemical that is poisonous only to insects leaks into the pond. It may only kill the insects directly, but there will probably not be enough food left for the small fish, frogs and insect-eating birds, and then there is no food for the larger predators either.

In this way energy from the sun, combined with basic nutrients from the earth, is made available through the whole animal kingdom.

Another name for grazers is herbivores ('plant-eaters'). Predators are also called carnivores ('flesh-eaters'). There are some animals which eat both vegetables and meat, like ourselves and badgers for instance, they are called omnivores ('everything-eaters').

Links

rivers and ponds
p.120

Recycling energy

Nothing goes to waste. The remains of dead plants and animals are eaten by another group of consumers – the detritivores ('eaters of worn-out stuff'). Worms, wood lice, toadstools, moulds and plenty of invisible *organisms* like bacteria, are all part of the decomposer food chain. The worms and slugs feed on the fragments of plant matter; the larvae of many flies feed on dead flesh. Moulds and bacteria feed on any remains and the waste of other creatures. So the last energy in organic material is extracted and any raw nutrients return to the soil. This is the energy cycle.

Links

(photosynthesis)
woodlands p.98

The waste problem

One of the main problems we are creating in the world today is the amount of waste we are leaving that cannot be broken down by nature's decomposers. All the plastics and other *synthetic* materials that we produce never existed in the world until recent years and there are no creatures or plants that can feed on them. Waste that can be decomposed by natural systems is said to be *biodegradable* ('bios' is the Greek word for life).

▼ Flea – a tiny insect that lives in animal fur.

Parasites

There is another kind of creature that feeds on other animals, but is not really a predator, since it does not normally kill the animal it feeds from. These are parasites and the animal on which they live is called their host.

Parasites usually live or attach themselves to the body of another animal and feed on it in various ways; they are usually much smaller than their hosts. Fleas, lice, ticks, the larvae of various insects, lamprey and leeches are all parasites. Doesn't it make you itch just thinking about them? There are even parasites in the plant world, including orchids that feed on other plants.

Working together

Links

feeding birds
p.97

Herbivores do not usually have to travel far to find their food; they tend to live in areas where there is an abundance. Often they feed in herds or flocks, since there is plenty of food to go round and there are more eyes in a herd to keep a look out for predators. If the food supply runs out, the whole herd moves elsewhere in search of another food supply. Cows and sheep are herbivores.

Finches are seed-eating birds that tend to live in flocks. Seeds are produced by different plants at different times, so it helps to have a number of birds together looking for a source of food they can all feed on.

▶ Wolves hunt as a team.

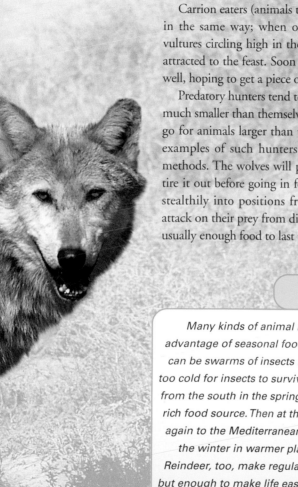

Carrion eaters (animals that feed on other dead animals) behave in the same way; when one vulture finds a dead sheep, other vultures circling high in the air see it going down to land and are attracted to the feast. Soon there will be a few ravens and crows as well, hoping to get a piece of the meal.

Predatory hunters tend to work alone and they usually take prey much smaller than themselves. But some species hunt in packs and go for animals larger than themselves. Wolves and lions are good examples of such hunters, though they have slightly different methods. The wolves will pursue a deer for some time aiming to tire it out before going in for the kill, whereas the lions will creep stealthily into positions from which they can launch a sudden attack on their prey from different directions. In both cases there is usually enough food to last the whole group for a few days.

Migration

Many kinds of animal make regular migrations to take advantage of seasonal food supplies. In northern Europe there can be swarms of insects in the summer, where in winter it is too cold for insects to survive. Countless numbers of birds arrive from the south in the spring to live and raise their young on this rich food source. Then at the end of summer they drift off south again to the Mediterranean, Africa and southern Asia to spend the winter in warmer places, where food is easier to find. Reindeer, too, make regular migrations, not as far as the birds, but enough to make life easier in winter. They spend the summer in the Arctic where there is a good growth of grasses and sedges in the long days. In winter they move further south to the edges of the forest areas, where it is more sheltered, though they still have to work quite hard to find food. If they had wings they would probably follow the birds even further south!

Storing food

▼ Red squirrel at work on the lawn.

Another way in which animals make the best of seasonal variations in their food supply is by storing up food when there is plenty of it (usually at the end of summer and into autumn). Jays, squirrels and nuthatches all collect ripe acorns in the autumn and hide them, so that they have something to rely on during the winter when food is hard to find. Jays have been found to have a fantastic memory for the hundreds of places they hide their acorns in. If you see a squirrel digging in your garden, there is a good chance it is either burying a nut or digging out one it has buried previously. Good for the squirrel, but it makes a mess of your lawn!

Pellets

▲ Owl pellets.

Many predators, when they eat their prey items, also consume much of the tougher parts of the animal, that aren't easily digested – beetle casing, eggshells, the fur and bones of small mammals and suchlike. Owls may swallow small rodents like mice and voles whole. They get rid of tougher materials by regurgitating them bunched together in a pellet. If you see a small sausage-shaped pellet of faded fur and bone, take a closer look; you could even prise it apart with a small twig. There may be something you can identify, such as a mouse's jawbone and teeth. Experts study the food of predators by analysing these pellets and identifying the pieces.

project

see a butterfly's suction at work

Butterflies have amazing mouth parts. During the summer months, watch out for a butterfly that comes in to land on a nearby flower. Try to get your head to the height of the flower, then gradually approach the butterfly, in slow motion – no sudden movements. You should see it roll out a long fine tube from beneath its eyes to suck the flower's juices.

Now the second part, the reward! Get a straw and a bottle of juice and imagine life as a butterfly, with a retractable straw for a mouth, sucking sweet juices on sunny days. One big difference is that the butterfly has no teeth like yours – so your juice should be low in sugar, so as not to rot them!

Links

butterflies p.63

▲ Red admiral feeding on ivy flower.

Defences – eat or be eaten

After finding food to provide energy, the next most important thing for an animal is to have some protection against being eaten by other animals and against extremes of weather.

Crabs and other crusties (*crustaceans*) have very hard skins to protect their soft bodies from getting bashed and to make it difficult for a predator to eat them. Snails and tortoises produce a hard outer shell into which they can withdraw when they are frightened. Mammals living in cold places usually have thick fur to keep them warm.

▲ Ground beetle – a tough and fast hunter of the insect world.

Some species of ground beetle have developed a way of dealing with snail shells that enables them to feed on snails. They have mouth-parts with sharp pincers that extend well in front of their heads, enabling them to get to the body of the snail through the shell's opening.

Several species of bird have also found ways of dealing with hard shells. Song thrushes use their beaks to hammer a whole snail on a rock, until the shell is in pieces and they can pick out the juicy meat: look for pieces of broken snail shells around rocks or any concrete and stone paths in your garden. Carrion crows, clever birds, pick hard-shelled mussels from coastal shores and drop them from a height onto rocks to smash them.

Speed and agility

For many animals speed is the main way to avoid capture; either a quick dash to cover, like a mouse running for a hole, or speed to out-distance any predator in a chase. Deer and hares rely on being able to run faster, for longer, than their attackers.

▲ Hares can turn quickly at high speed.

Hares have refined this method; they don't run in a straight line, but in a zig-zag pattern, making sudden dashing turns that leave any animal in pursuit scrambling to follow them. Sadly for hares that stray onto roads, they also try to throw off cars in this way, at least until they get to one of their runs through the hedge or under a gate. Many birds and insects use this technique to escape danger.

This method is taken one step further by massed creatures like flocks of birds or shoals of fish. They *synchronise* their movements so well that it seems like the whole crowd turns at once; this is thought to confuse predators, especially when the animals have striped markings which make it difficult for a predator to focus on an individual.

So the pressure is on the predator to be even faster, or more cunning in some way, if it is to catch its prey. Large cats, like cheetahs and lynx, aim to catch their prey by creeping close, then a very fast dash. Falcons are among the fastest flyers of the bird world and catch their prey, mainly other birds, in the air.

Other tricks

When a family of young birds is threatened, often the mother will start flapping her wings awkwardly nearby and calling as if she is injured. This is to attract the attention of the intruder and make her look like an easier catch than her young – when the intruder comes towards her, she flutters a little further off. It's called a distraction display, since it distracts a predator from the vulnerable young.

Grass snakes are one of many animals that 'play dead'. When a predator attacks, the grass snake sometimes rolls on its back with its mouth open, looking like it is dead. It is a last chance gamble, when a creature knows it is caught: it hopes the predator will lose interest and wander off.

Weapons

Spines, horns, stings, poisons, claws and fangs all help animals and plants to defend themselves. But they also become weapons of attack for predators hunting for food and in disputes over territories.

Spines

The fur of hedgehogs and porcupines has evolved into stiff spikes which is enough to discourage most predators. Whereas hedgehogs curl up into a spiky ball if threatened, many porcupines will charge at any would-be predator – in reverse, with their spiny back first. There are disadvantages to having spines instead of fur though; cleaning is difficult and hedgehogs usually carry many parasites, especially fleas, among their spines. Sea-urchins are covered in spines that act as a defence and help them to move.

▲ Hedgehogs are protected by a coat of spikes.

Thorns are a common defence in the plant world. Champions of the thorn league are gorse bushes, which grow in a dense mass of stiff, sharp spikes. Brambles have curved thorns that not only act as a defence, but help the plant scramble over other plants and grow higher.

Chemical weapons

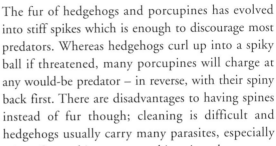
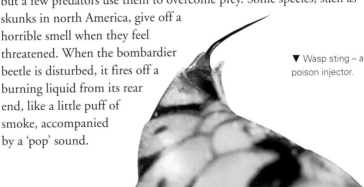

Other species have developed chemical weapons, mainly for defence, but a few predators use them to overcome prey. Some species, such as skunks in north America, give off a horrible smell when they feel threatened. When the bombardier beetle is disturbed, it fires off a burning liquid from its rear end, like a little puff of smoke, accompanied by a 'pop' sound.

◀◆▶

Links

safety p.188

▼ Wasp sting – a poison injector.

Poisons are complex substances produced by many different plants and animals that affect the body chemistry of other animals, sometimes killing them. Some species taste horrible or may be poisonous when eaten. The trouble with this is that the predator only finds out, after it has eaten its victim – too late for the victim (as well as the predator!). The plant or animal needs somehow to warn any potential predators that it tastes horrible or is poisonous, so that the predator doesn't eat it; this is why many poisonous creatures are brightly coloured.

Some kinds of frog and toad have poisons in their skin – but not the species of northern Europe. The hairs of some large caterpillars have chemicals that irritate our skin. Plants also use chemical defences: the brittle hairs of stinging nettles have a chemical that's painful when it gets under our skin. The tentacles of many jellyfish can give very nasty stings.

Those species that are more aggressive with their poisons need some way of injecting it into their attackers (or in the case of some snakes and spiders, their prey); they do this with bites and stings. Stings are usually in the tail of an animal, though some have poisonous spines – particularly some species of fish.

Traps

Spiders are the champions when it comes to trapping prey. Somehow they have evolved with the ability to spin sticky threads and the skill to weave their threads into nets with various patterns. The most visible are the webs spread across gaps in plants, designed to catch small flies. The spider waits in cover at the edge of the web and rushes out when it feels the vibrations of struggling prey. Sometimes you can fool a spider into coming out by gently shaking a very small twig on the centre of the web.

Links

spiders p.70

◀ Spider's web – a fly trap.

Mimicry

▲ A hoverfly; notice it doesn't have a narrow waist like a wasp.

▼ Bee orchid.

There is another clever trick that's useful in the fight to survive – *mimicry*. Camouflage is a simple kind of mimicry, where the colour patterns and shape of an animal help it blend with its surroundings. Females of many bird species have dull colours and broken patterns so that they are not easy to see when sitting on a nest. But it also works for predators: stick insects keep very still and look just like part of the twig they are resting on, until some prey insect comes within reach. Then they suddenly lunge forward with their long arms to grab their victim. Chameleons are unusual in that they can change the colour of their skin to match their surroundings.

There are also harmless species that do very well out of looking just like poisonous or stinging animals. There are some species of hoverflies, harmless fast-flying insects that look just like wasps and bees.

Many insects, particularly butterflies and moths, have eye-like markings on their wings. This is designed to confuse a predator for a brief moment into thinking there is a larger animal here. The large caterpillar of the elephant hawkmoth takes this a step further. Not only does it have eye-like markings, but when threatened it sways its front end in the air to look like the head of a small snake. It is very effective – the lady who found this caterpillar in her garden thought it was a snake!

▼ Elephant hawkmoth caterpillar – *c.*6cm long.

There are also plants that produce flowers that look just like insects, such as the bee orchid. But this type of mimicry is actually to attract insects, rather than for defensive purposes.

Meet the natives

Birds

Divers, grebes, albatrosses, herons, geese, ducks, eagles, hawks, falcons, grouse, pheasants, rails, waders, gulls, terns, auks, doves, owls, woodpeckers, larks, swallows, martins, pipits, wagtails, chats, thrushes, warblers, flycatchers, tits, shrikes, crows, sparrows, finches, buntings.

▲ Archaeopterix – the first birds looked something like this.

Although birds have evolved into many different kinds (over 9,000 species in the world) and they can live in all the habitats of the earth, from the poles to the tropics, birds generally all conform to the same design. This is because the stream-lined shape is needed for efficient flying. Birds are the living descendents of dinosaurs and masters of the air.

Imagine what it is like to float on the wind. The power to fly gives birds the kind of freedom we can only imagine; and it gives them a quick escape at the approach of danger and so they can live their lives more in the open. They can also travel large distances quickly. There are some species that don't fly well though and a few not at all.

Birds are very alert creatures, with good sight and hearing, but don't seem to have a good sense of smell. They communicate with each other well, using both sound and visual signals. Birds have some of the most elaborate song and dance rituals of the animal world. Spring is the time when males tend to pose and show off to each other to attract females. Bird song is all a part of this show.

Links

bird song – using your ears p.153

Nature Safari

Many species are very sociable: as the saying goes, 'birds of a feather flock together'. Flocks are often of the same species ('of a feather' meaning 'with the same feathers'), but different species also regularly mix together. Though some species of bird breed together in colonies, pairs of most like to have their own territory to nest in. They will defend this from other members of their species and sometimes fast chases and fights break out. After breeding, many then gather in flocks again for the winter.

Since flight also enables birds to travel long distances, they can make the best of seasonal food supplies: spending summer in the north and winter in the warmth further south (relative to Europe). They are the great migrants of the earth's land creatures. Arctic terns travel almost the length of the earth and back each year. Born in northern Europe, they travel right down to Antarctic seas in the southern hemisphere in the winter. Then back again to breed next spring. So, for a bird that is almost constantly on the move, where is its home?

Feathers are the secret to birds' powers of flight. It is thought that they evolved from scales, as birds evolved from reptiles. Relative to their weight, feathers are one of the strongest materials known; so a bird can have large wings and a protective covering of feathers without increasing its weight too much. Feathers are made from keratin – the same substance as hair, claws (including our finger nails) and horns. The quill, which is almost like a backbone to a feather, is hollow, but rigid.

▲ Light as a feather.

▼ Swallow 'preening' – birds spend time keeping their feathers in good shape.

The largest birds in Europe are mute swans and great bustards, but these don't fly often. The largest European birds that spend a lot of time in the air are vultures, closely followed by eagles. The smallest European bird is the goldcrest, which can often be seen in gardens and parks; it prefers coniferous trees.

Usually the males of a species are more brightly coloured than the females, but not always. There are some species, such as dotterel, where the females are the more colourful and the males rear the family. Some birds' feathering provides them with superb camouflage in their habitats.

▲ Birds take great care of their eggs.

There are some species of bird that live their lives on the ground and are unable to fly, such as ostriches which are large and can run very fast. Penguins' wings are too short for flying, but work very well for swimming underwater. Their European relatives, razorbills and guillemots , just manage to fly, but have to flap their wings very rapidly.

Birds, like insects and most reptiles and amphibians, lay eggs. Most species build intricately-woven, and usually well-hidden, nests to protect and keep their eggs warm. The parents also sit on the eggs in the nest to keep them warm. The egg needs warmth for the young chick to develop and hatch. The parents then work very hard to provide food for their family, since the young need to grow a full set of flight feathers and be able to leave the nest really very quickly. From hatching to fledging can be anything from three weeks in the case of small birds to eleven weeks for birds like eagles. It takes humans at least 16 years!

If you see a bird carrying grass, feathers or a twig in its beak, it is almost certainly building a nest. If you see one carrying food, like worms or flies and other insects, it probably has a nest with young nearby. If you do find a nest, don't stay too long near it – you may cause the parents to desert it. And try not to disturb the vegetation around it: if predators like magpies or cats find the nest that will be the end of it and anything in it.

Nature Safari

Links

garden birds
p.96
special events
p.186

◀ Where there are trees nearby great spotted woodpeckers will visit peanut feeders.

To see birds at their best

Feed the birds in your garden during the winter

Take a boat trip to an island seabird colony during the breeding season

Visit a good wetlands site on a bright winter day

Listen to the dawn chorus early on a May morning

Linger into the twilight on a heathland in summer

Look out for unusual migrants passing through parks in the autumn

Visit a hide to see something special, like an osprey's nest or a black grouse lek

Mammals

Shrews, mice, bats, voles, rats, weasels, stoats, hedgehogs, rabbits, hares, badgers, foxes, otters, deer, seals, porpoises, dolphins, whales.

▲ Foxes are general predators, living in all kinds of habitats.

Mammals tend to be furry creatures and are the group of animals to which we humans belong. The special feature of mammals is that they give birth to living young (rather than eggs), which are fed at first by milk from the mother.

◄ Field vole – one of the commonest mammals of the countryside: it is mainly nocturnal and is a prey item for many different predators.

Mammals can grow to large sizes: elephants, giraffes and bison are all mammals. But some are tiny, such as shrews: the pygmy shrews of Europe aren't much bigger than a 50 pence piece with a short tail.

Mostly they are earthbound and at least the smaller kinds tend to be timid, scurrying creatures of the night. Also nocturnal in lifestyle are the bats, but bats have taken to the air. Some mammals have taken to the sea. Seals, walruses with their great tusks, dolphins and whales are all mammals and need to return to the surface at intervals to breathe.

► Female grey seal threatening an intruder.

Nature Safari

The largest land mammals in Europe are bison (just a few left in Poland) and elk in northern and eastern Europe. There are a few brown bears left in some mountain forests, but none in Britain. These can grow very large. The largest mammal in Britain is the red deer. They are quite numerous in the Scottish Highlands, but only a few remain in southern Britain; the New Forest, Exmoor and a few parks are the best places.

Deer

Red deer males are known as stags and the females as hinds; the stags grow a large set of antlers (branching horns) each year. The old ones fall off in the spring and new ones grow over the summer ready for the autumn rut when the stags begin to challenge each other. They roar and shake their heads at each other and just occasionally end up head-to-head in a fight.

Roe deer are the commonest and most widespread deer; the males, known as bucks, grow a set of short, but sharply-pointed antlers. Young bucks just have spikes. Fallow deer are lighter in colouring and have quite dappled coats. The muntjac deer, introduced into Britain from Asia, is only the size of a dog and it barks like one. Deer are all herbivores.

▼ Deer cast off their old antlers in the spring: if you're lucky you may find one. Red deer – above, fallow – below

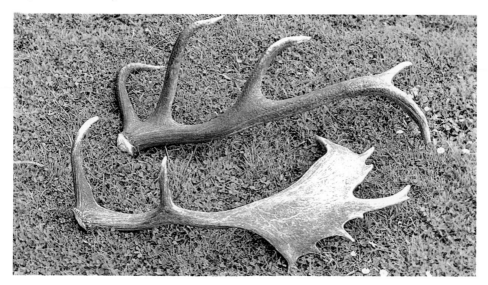

Shrews

Relative to its size, the tiny shrew is one of the fiercest creatures of the animal kingdom. It is a very active carnivore, that needs to eat frequently, so it is almost constantly hunting for worms, beetles and suchlike. Shrews are quite common in most areas, but live on the ground in thick vegetation, so aren't seen too often. It is easier to hear them than see them – if you are young. They make a very high-pitched squeaking, so high-pitched that older people have difficulty hearing it. If you have a cat, it may have brought in a shrew that it caught. You can recognise them by their small size and long, pointed nose.

Moles

▼ Mole – adapted to life underground.

Moles are small mammals that live in underground tunnels. They have very poor eyesight, since the their world is quite dark, but their sense of smell is good. If you ever get the chance to see a mole close up, take a look at its front paws. They are very powerful for an animal of this size, with tough claws, ideal for all the digging it does. You know when there's been a mole about by the heaps of soil in trails across the grass – 'molehills'.

Nature Safari

Bats

Bats are the only kind of mammal to take to the air; some kinds of squirrel can glide, but bats are proper fliers. They have a thin webbing of skin stretched between elongated fingers to form wings. They are mostly nocturnal, though can sometimes be seen flying by day. The European species are mostly quite small and feed on insects which they catch in flight. In tropical regions there are large fruit-eating bats (also called 'flying foxes'), bats that hunt small rainforest frogs and blood-sucking vampire bats. Scary? Not at all, they feed mostly on the ankles of cows and goats – still a bit unpleasant though!

Like dolphins and some whales, bats use bleeps of sound for hunting, in a process known as echo location. A hunting bat sends out a series of short, very high-pitched clicks, as it flies around; these clicks bounce off anything nearby and the bat hears the echo. The clever part is that the bat cannot only hear when a moth or other insect comes into range, but hears precisely where it is. Just as we can see, echo-location is the bat's night vision. And that is why a bat is unlikely to bump into you, even in the dark.

▲ The large ears of this bat help it 'see' in the darkness.

But it seems that moths are not entirely defenceless: they hear or feel the bat's sharp clicking sound and have learnt to dive quickly towards the ground – hopefully out of the bat's flight path. And I've been told that if you make a sharp clicking noise by hitting a piece of metal, any moths nearby will drop to the ground. I haven't tried it; maybe you can. Make sure you can see a few moths flying nearby that might hear the sound.

Badger watch

Links

special events
p.186
approaching wild
creatures p.143
animal tracks
and signs p.146

The badger, sometimes known as a 'brock', may resemble a low, slouching dog, but it is actually a small bear that goes on all four legs. It eats all manner of things from the roots of plants, berries and fruit to insects, worms, bird's eggs and small mammals. Badgers are quite sociable creatures, sleeping and resting underground together in family groups in dens, known as setts.

They are generally timid animals, avoiding a fight; but when they are cornered, they fight fiercely, using their strong jaws and claws. They are also very clean animals. They regularly change the dry grasses that they use for bedding in their setts (one of the signs of a badger sett). They dig little holes (latrines) away from the sett to use for a toilet; and family members spend time cleaning fleas and ticks from each others' fur (known as 'grooming').

▲ When they're very hungry, badgers may come out in daylight.

TIP • TIP • TIP

• If a hedgehog starts to visit your garden, don't put out bread and milk for it – these are not good for its digestion. Try a little tinned pet food or some scraps of meat and water.
• If you spot an otter in water and it dives, you should be able to follow its progress by the trail of bubbles at the surface.
• Learn to recognise the smell of a fox – sweet and musty.

Badgers are generally only active at night, though in summer, when the nights are short, they are out and about in the late evening and early morning. And these are the best times to go on a badger watch. You need to be aware of the wind direction: badgers don't see very well (this may be why they often wear glasses in cartoons), but their sense of smell is excellent.

You will need to be in your watching place near a sett before the animals emerge, so get there before sunset. And you will need plenty of patience, since you will have to wait VERY quietly: badgers have also got very good hearing.

Nature Safari

Amphibians and reptiles

Snakes, lizards, tortoises, crocodiles, frogs, toads, newts, salamanders

We humans have divided feelings about these animals: in our stories we often make them out to be evil and many people are afraid to even touch one, yet we are fascinated by them and many keep reptiles as pets (some of whom don't look after them as well as they should!). These are ancient forms of animal: one group of their descendants, the dinosaurs, has evolved and become extinct since some amphibians first took up life on dry land and evolved into reptiles.

There is one big difference between ourselves and these creatures: their bodies cannot generate their own heat. They need the warmth of the sun to bring them up to a good operating temperature. And so you find that the further north you go, the fewer reptiles and amphibians there are.

▲ Dinosaurs are an extinct family of reptiles.

The reptiles that do live in the cooler, northern regions tend to spend the cold months of the winter in a state of *hibernation* – a deep sleep, where all the processes of the body slow down. When the first sunny days of spring come, these northern snakes and lizards spend much time basking in a sheltered sunny spot, warming their bodies up. At this time the animals are sluggish and slow to respond to danger, so it is a good time to look for them in the right places. But be careful in adder country: their bite is deadly poisonous.

Reptiles

Reptiles (the word 'reptile' means 'creeping', as with your belly to the ground) like to sunbathe to warm themselves up; but they then return to the shade when it is very hot, so that they don't overheat. Because they don't use energy in warming up their bodies, reptiles don't need to eat so frequently as mammals or birds. As well as being *cold-blooded,* they're mostly silent.

▲ Slow-worm – a harmless reptile sometimes found in gardens.

Usually lizards have legs and snakes do not. But there are some odd lizards that have very small legs and the slow-worm, although it looks like a small snake, is actually a legless lizard. They are almost all predators and each type has some senses sharp enough to hunt their prey well and detect danger.

Reptiles' skin is covered in small scales, which give them a shiny appearance. They are dry and not at all slimy.

Snakes

Snakes have poor eyesight, but they can detect movement quite well. Although they don't have ears and can't hear sounds, they are sensitive to vibrations in the earth or tree they are lying on. So the stories of snakes being hypnotised by the tunes of snake-charmers' flutes are not quite accurate; it is probably the movements of the snake-charmer that captivate the snake.

Some snakes, such as rattlesnakes, have a special sense tuned to the temperature around them and they can detect a creature of prey from the warmth of its body. But in general the most important senses for snakes are smell and taste. When you see a snake flicking out its tongue, it is actually tasting the air for the scent of prey or danger.

Adders are found further north in Europe than any other snake. Like rattlesnakes, they have traditional underground dens that get used regularly for hibernation; they need to remain dry and get the best of what little warmth there is. When many snakes gather at the same site, they all hibernate together and this may help a little with warmth. Maybe this is the origin of the idea of a snake-pit.

▲ Adder – note the dark zig-zag marking on it's back.

Snakes kill their prey in one of two ways: they either have a pair of fangs with which to deliver a venomous bite, or they suffocate their victim by squeezing it in gradually tightening curls of their body. The larger snakes around the world all tend to be constrictors that suffocate their prey.

The safest course is to keep a good distance from a snake, unless you know for sure which species it is and that it is not venomous. Adders usually slither off for cover when they sense a person approaching. Most humans are bitten when they accidentally step on, sit on or put their hand on a snake without seeing it. The snake thinks it is being attacked and bites back. So you should never approach one too close.

Amphibians and reptiles

Snakes are not generally common in northern Europe and adders are the only venomous species; there are more dangerous species in southern Europe. Snakebites are rare in Europe, but if someone does get bitten, they will need to get medical attention as soon as possible.

Genesis, the first book of the Bible, tells the story of the first man and woman – Adam and Eve. They lived in an innocent paradise called the Garden of Eden, until one day Eve was tempted to take a bite from the apple of knowledge. And who was the wicked agent who tempted her? A snake – surprised? It just shows how long humans have regarded snakes as their enemies.

Why do you think people fear and hate snakes? If you are careful and respect the snake, you should have no problem. It is quite something to look into the eye of a wild snake.

Grass snakes are a beautiful, harmless species that can grow up to 1.5m. They are widespread in Europe, except for the far north. They like damp meadows and ditches. When they are alarmed they sometimes roll onto their backs and pretend to be dead. Where gardens border onto meadows and streams, gardeners sometimes find grass snake eggs in their compost heaps.

Lizards

The largest lizard in the world is the Komodo dragon, which grows to 3m in length, is surprisingly quick and agile and has been known to attack humans. Fortunately they are only found on a few islands in the south Pacific. The largest lizard in Europe, the ocellated lizard, grows to about 50cm. Lizards have good eyesight. Did you know dinosaurs are named from the Greek words 'dino', meaning fearsome, and 'saurus', meaning lizard?

The common lizard, which is often found on some heaths and moors, has a trick in its tail for escaping a close encounter with a predator. They grow long tails with a weak bone-joint near where the tail joins the rest of the body. This means that their tails can break off quite easily; another, blunter tail grows in time, but not as long as the original. Well, from the lizard's point of view, it is better to escape less one tail than to end up as breakfast for a buzzard – tail and all. So if you try to catch a lizard, don't grab it by the tail.

Nature Safari

project

fishing for lizards

If you find a place where a lizard regularly runs for cover, there is a way of tempting it into the open. You will need a fishing rod and a trout fly. Ask an adult to snip the hook off the trout fly with pliers. Creep up carefully, then sit quietly to the side and dangle the fly on the end of the line in front of where you think the lizard hides. If you are patient, the lizard should come and grab the fly in its mouth. That is why you take the hook off, so as not to damage the lizard's mouth.

▲ A lizard from southern Europe.

Amphibians

Links

wildlife
gardening
(amphibians)
p.92
meadows,
heaths and
moors (reptiles)
p.132

Amphibians lead double lives, partly *aquatic* and partly *terrestrial*. Adults lay their eggs in water and the young tadpoles, when they hatch, live and breath in water. After several months they grow into the adult forms, which breathe air, but still spend time in or around water.

In the colder, northern winters the adults spend the winter in a *dormant* state buried in mud or sheltered under a log. In milder southern sites they may be active during the winter.

In the spring, when the daily temperature rises enough, the adults begin to return to their breeding ponds. Some species, such as the common toad, tend to winter away from the breeding ponds and may have some distance to travel. They tend to make their journeys at night, sometimes in large numbers. They are safer at night, though owls take some and many die under the wheels of cars, if their pond is near a road.

So early spring is a good time to look for frogs and toads, gathered in groups in pond edges or marshy pools. On a warm day, especially a mild evening, listen for the choruses of the males singing to attract females. Frogs species tend to make drawn-out croaks and toads short squeaky sounds or whoops.

▲ Great crested newt.

▼ Common toad.

Newts are silent. The males try to attract females with a kind of dance where they curl their tail and make it shiver. This also wafts their scent to the female. Male newts have bright patterns on their bellies.

Toads have rough or warty-looking skin, whereas the skin of frogs is fairly smooth. Another difference between frogs and toads is that toads crawl, whereas frogs move in a series of leaps. You can tell toad spawn from frog spawn, since it is laid in strings, usually hanging from pond plants, whereas frog spawn is just laid in a mass.

project

raising frog spawn

It is not too difficult to raise some frog spawn into young frogs at home or school. You need as big a water container as you can find. If you have access to a pond in your garden, even a small one, that's much better. If you are using a large jar or tank remember to change some of the water occasionally, so it doesn't get too dirty. Use either pond water or rain water if you can.

▲ Common frogs and spawn.

Frog spawn usually takes about three weeks from laying to hatching; you can see the progress as the round black dot in the centre of each egg slowly turns into a comma shape as it grows a tail. The free-swimming tadpole at first has small feathery gills then is just head and tail. Gradually it grows back legs then front legs and the tail gets smaller. Once they've hatched, you'll need to add some food to the tank, such as pieces of soft green leaves.

It takes about three to four months from hatching for the tadpoles to develop fully into little frogs able to breathe in the air. If you have raised them in a tank away from their natural environment of marsh and pond, you will have to think about releasing them somewhere – ideally where you found the frog spawn.

The needs of a frog are different from a tadpole. Tadpoles can survive in the enclosed world of a tank of water, feeding on plant matter in the water. As frogs they eat insects, and have a need to wander in search of food.

Do not try to keep adult frogs, toads or newts in a tank. They need plenty of space on dry land for their hunting. If you want to see more of these amphibians (and who doesn't?), persuade your parents that your garden needs a pond. Now there's a challenge!

Insects and spiders

Spring-tails, dragonflies, stoneflies, grasshoppers, cockroaches, earwigs, bugs, aphids, fleas, lacewings, butterflies, moths, caddis flies, mosquitoes, midges, horse-flies, hoverflies, house flies, ants, wasps, bees, beetles, centipedes, ticks, scorpions, harvestmen, spiders.

Insects, spiders, millipedes and *crustaceans* are part of the group of animals known as *arthropods*. These are *invertebrates*, which means they don't have a backbone; instead they have a rigid body casing, with flexible joints.

Insects normally have six legs in three pairs and most insects have wings at some stage of their life. Spiders have eight legs. Insects have been around for a long time, almost 400 million years (well before dinosaurs), so they are a very successful group of animals. Although primitive life develops in many ways, they have evolved some complex behaviour patterns and ways of communicating with each other.

Swarming

▲ Foxgloves: flowers provide food for many insects.

Insects are the most numerous visible animal on earth and there are many, many different kinds, around 10,000 in Britain and 100,000 in Europe alone. Identifying them all is usually a job for an expert. But it is quite easy to get to know the different families. Flies and beetles are probably the most familiar. Most beetles actually fly too, but their wings are covered by their back casing when at rest. Caterpillars and maggots are the young, or *larvae*, of insects.

Nature Safari

Insects are very important to flowering plants, despite the fact that caterpillars and other larvae often eat their leaves. Plants grow brightly-coloured flowers to attract adult insects to the sweet liquids within; as insects move from one plant to another, they spread pollen between their different flowers and the plant's seeds become *fertile*.

Daddy long-legs is a common name for the crane flies that can be plentiful in summer, buzzing around erratically, long legs dangling. The female has a pointed tip to the rear of her body – for egg-laying, it is not a sting. They are not good fliers and easily bump into you. Some people also call large harvestmen (related to spiders) daddy long-legs because they look similar.

Larger beetles also make clumsy fliers and sometimes bump into people and cling to clothes. This is accidental – they are not chasing you!

▲ Daddy long-legs.

Ladybirds are pretty and harmless and make a welcome insect in any garden. Their larvae feed on aphids like greenfly – tiny insects that can become a pest on garden plants.

◀ Ladybird –its tough, spotted back acts as a casing to protect its wings.

Commonly known as mayflies, the adults of many different species look similar: beautiful, harmless flies often found near water.

Catching insects

A traditional butterfly net, also called a 'sweep net', is best for flying insects. It has a short handle, a wide net opening and quite a deep net of fine, light-weight, but tough mesh. Most fishing nets aren't suitable and are more likely to damage the insects you are trying to catch.

Some kind of specimen jar is essential: something you can keep an insect or two in for a short time while you observe them. You can buy inexpensive, clear plastic ones, with a magnifying glass in the lid and small breathing holes around the edge. Or you could adapt a jam jar. Remember the holes for breathing; don't keep anything in the jar for too long and don't leave it in hot sunshine.

Pit-fall trap

A good way of catching the insects and other creepy-crawlies that spend their time on the ground, is with a pit-fall trap. Get a small, steep-sided jar and bury it in the ground wherever you think will be a good place. Make sure to pack the soil carefully back around it to the jar's rim. Then leave it for an hour or two – or even overnight.

You can put a board over it resting on stones; make sure there is room underneath for things to get in. Insects that fall in will not be able to get back out, unless they can fly; glass is just too smooth for their feet to grasp onto. Make sure you let your catch go, once you've examined it.

Make a note of what you catch in your diary – with a drawing of anything unusual. If you do this on a regular basis, putting the trap in the same place and noting your catch, you should learn a lot about the life of different insects. And you can bet that one morning something unusual will be in your jar that will really puzzle you. Nature is unpredictable.

Nature Safari

Dragonflies

Hover – dash – hover. Rattling wings. Flashes of colour. And up close, two enormous *iridescent* eyes. These are the impressions of an encounter with northern Europe's most spectacular insect.

▲ Dragonfly warming up in the sun.

They are most frequently found near water, since the first stages of their lives, egg and larva, are as water creatures. Then one summer day (you may see this if you have a pond), the larva climbs a reed, its outer skin dries in the open air and a beautiful monstrous flying-machine emerges – the adult dragonfly.

In both active stages of their lives dragonflies prey on other insects: as larvae they also prey on small fish and tadpoles, but as adults their food is almost exclusively insects, which they catch in a swift aerial chase. Each hunting dragonfly has a limited territory it patrols, hovering at intervals to look out for prey (or rival dragonflies intruding into its territory). Hence the hover-dash-hover way of flying.

Why do you think they are called dragonflies? Well, they may not breathe fire, but on the smaller scale of the insect world, they are

enormous flying monsters, predators to be avoided. Different families include the hawkers, the darters and the chasers. Damselflies are very like dragonflies, but usually smaller, with thinner bodies, and they close their wings over their backs at rest, whereas dragonflies hold theirs out.

The largest dragonflies now have a wingspan of about 15cm. But dragonflies are an ancient insect and back in the fern forests of 300 million years ago, there were dragonflies with wingspans of nearly 1m.

▲ Damselfly

▶ Dragonflies hunt by sight and have large eyes.

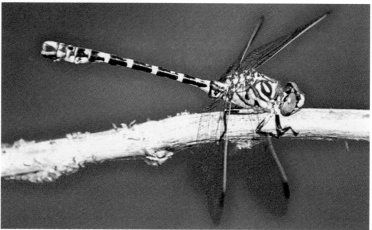

TIP • TIP • TIP • TIP • TIP • TIP • TIP • TIP • TIP • TIP • TIP

• If you can be patient and keep still in an area where a large hawker is patrolling, it should soon come up close to have a look at you. They tend to patrol a regular circuit, returning to the same spot every minute or two. And they are harmless to humans – there is no sting in their tail.

• When a dragonfly catches its prey, it lands somewhere nearby to eat it. They can be approached quite close while they are busy eating – if you move slowly. You can then watch, and maybe even hear, its massive jaws (relatively speaking!) crunching up the other insect. In the insect world, they really are prehistoric monsters.

Butterflies and moths

These insects are known as *lepidoptera* by scientists. It comes from the Greek words for wings ('ptera') and scales ('lepido'). Yes – the Greeks really did begin words with 'pt'. Pterodactyl means with winged fingers.

It is their wings that distinguish them from other groups of insects and wow – what wings! The bold or intricate, colourful patterns on the wings make some of these creatures contenders for the beauty crown in the insect world. But this is just the adult stage of their life.

Adults lay eggs in spring and summer which hatch into caterpillars. The caterpillars feed greedily on vegetable matter; many have specific food plants. When they are well-fed, they turn into a *chrysalis* or *pupa*: butterflies produce a hard case hanging from a plant, moths often spin a cocoon. In this state the caterpillar undergoes a *metamorphosis* into the adult insect, sometimes not until the winter has passed. Adults feed mostly on the sugary juices of flowers.

▲ Peacock butterfly.

► White admiral.

▲ Tiger moth caterpillar: like many caterpillars, it curls up when frightened.

Links

butterfly feeding,
see finding food
p.35

Butterflies fly by day and can close their wings upright above their backs; usually the underwing is better camouflaged than the boldly marked upper side of the wings. Moths cannot do this, but most can close their forewings over their backwings and they generally fly at night. Many species of both butterflies and moths have eye-like markings on their wings; this is to startle predators, who think they are the eyes of a larger creature.

▲ The Hawkmoth family includes this spectacular eyed hawkmoth.

Moths are attracted to lights: you can often find unusual ones attracted to your windows at night. Try not drawing the curtains. The family with the most spectacular wings is the hawkmoths. They aren't common and prefer the warmer regions of Europe, but with research or luck you could see one.

Moths can also be attracted by putting out food for them. Dissolve a few spoonfuls of sugar or syrup in a little warm water, until you have a very sticky solution. Paint some patches of this on a tree trunk, some branches, logs, rocks or a wall and you should find that moths and other insects are drawn to the supply of sweet food.

Links

for making your
garden butterfly-
friendly, see
wildlife
gardening p.92

Try not to touch the wings of butterflies and moths, since the tiny scales that cover the wings rub off very easily.

You can raise caterpillars into butterflies; but you need to identify what their food plant is. Unless you observed the caterpillar munching away on a leaf, this probably means you need to identify the caterpillar. Keep them in a large container with small air holes and plenty of fresh food. You will need to clean it out when it becomes messy with their droppings. When eventually the adult butterflies emerge you should release them back into the wild.

Good places for butterflies

Coastal dunes
Flower meadows
Woodland glades and edges
Bramble patches in flower
Buddleia bushes and thistles

project

make a butterfly kite

You will need:

Paper   Sticky tape
Straws   Pipe cleaner
String   Pens/crayons
Scissors

1. Draw the wings and body on plain paper. Make the wings around 15cm tall with a 15cm wing span. The body should be around 8cm tall. Colour the wings with whatever pattern and colours you like – it could be the same as your favourite butterfly or something from your imagination.

2. Cut out the wings (making sure they are joined in the middle) and the body.

3. Glue the body to the middle of the wings.

4. Cut two small antennae from a pipe cleaner and glue to the head.

5. Lay a piece of string (around 50cm in length) along the body of the butterfly.

6. Place two straws over the string in an 'X' shape and tape them down at the corners of the wings.

7. Tie the string firmly around the straws.

Your kite is now ready for the air – hold on tightly to the string and run!

▲ Butterflies also make good designs for masks.

Grasshoppers and crickets

Links

dunes p.114
using your ears
p.153

Grasshoppers and crickets, are close relations – rather like cousins. They are solidly built, rather sturdy insects and some species grow quite large. The mole cricket and a few other European types can grow up to 5cms in length; and some tropical species grow much bigger. But most of those found in Britain and northern Europe are about 2–3cm long.

They have big eyes and lengthy antennae. They also have a very large pair of hind-legs which provide them with the ability to make a quick get-away when danger threatens. They make a sudden leap into the air and then spread their wings to fly off several metres. Imagine if you could jump from a stand-still to twenty times your height!

Many species of grasshopper have brightly coloured hind wings, so can be seen clearly when they fly off, but when they close their wings and drop to the ground, their camouflaged colouring helps them disappear from sight.

Grasshoppers and crickets have powerful jaws and the larger species, such as the great green bush-cricket can give quite a painful bite when handled – so watch out! Grasshoppers are mostly vegetarian, but many of the crickets also eat other insects.

▼ Bush-cricket.

You may spot an individual with a vicious-looking spike as a tail: don't worry, this isn't a sting, but a tool to help with egg-laying. Many people think that grasshoppers and crickets look rather strange – in fact they have provided the inspiration for monsters in some horror films.

project

watch grasshoppers sing

The males of many species 'sing' to attract females. It's a mechanical kind of singing produced by rubbing one part of the body against another; grasshoppers usually rub their hind legs against their stiff front wings. Each species has its own kind of song; some sound like sewing machines, others like short bursts of scraping or ticking.

If you get down low and creep up quietly on a singing grasshopper, so as not to frighten it, you should be able to see its legs vibrating to produce the sound. Musicians have percussion instruments that work in the same way to produce fast rhythmic sounds.

▲ Grasshopper

Finding them

The sound of their singing is probably the best clue for finding grasshoppers. Otherwise, if you are walking through meadow grasses, watch out for large insects jumping out as you approach and then drifting off for a few metres. Once they have landed you will have to look and listen carefully as they can be well camouflaged.

When and where

Grasshoppers can be found throughout Britain whereas crickets are only found in the southern parts of the country. They both live in the long grass of meadows (not lawns or close-cropped fields). They can also be found in the mixed grasses of heaths and moors and in patches of grass on sand dunes. Woodland clearings can also be good for them.

You will only find them during the summer months. This is because the adults do not live through the winter. They lay their eggs in the summer and then die. The eggs hatch in late spring and the youngsters, known as nymphs, emerge. They soon grow into adults and the cycle begins again.

Grasshoppers are active on warm sunny days, so this is the best time to try and spot them. Crickets vary – some species are active on sunny days whereas others are nocturnal and sing during the night.

TIP • TIP • TIP

• A small paint brush is very useful for picking up small insects; bring the hairs of the brush gently up to the insect so that it has to climb onto the brush.

legendary

The wart-biter cricket

Guess how the wart-biter got its name? Yes, it is said that once upon a time people used this insect to bite warts off their skin. They probably thought the insect had some magical power to stop the wart reappearing, as warts tend to do. The wart-biter is now very rare in Britain, but is more common further south in Europe.

Nature Safari

Bees and wasps

These insects are well known as stingers – very painful and dangerous for some people with weak hearts or an allergy to their venom. Fortunately their wings produce a loud buzzing noise, so you can usually hear them approaching. But they only sting when they feel threatened. In fact bees die after using their sting, which is left in their victim, so it is something only used in desperation. Wasps can use their sting again if they manage to escape.

Most bee stings probably happen when someone sits down in grass on a bee feeding on a flower. The bee struggles to gain flight and panics into using its ultimate defence. Many wasp stings happen when people accidentally step on the entrance to a wasps' nest or in the autumn when wasps are becoming drowsy and come indoors looking for somewhere to *hibernate*.

▲ Wasps are attracted to sweet foods, like a ripe apple.

But there is another very interesting thing about wasps and bees (and their close relatives, ants): the commoner species live in large colonies like cities. They are referred to as social insects and, within their colony, different groups have different jobs.

A bee colony has a queen, workers and drones. There is only one queen and her role is to lay all the eggs for the colony. All the other females are workers, collecting food, building the honeycomb in the centre of the nest and looking after the eggs. The males are known as 'drones' and their job is to fertilise the queen's eggs. Later when they no longer have any job to do, they may be driven off by the workers.

Bees, with their hairy legs, are important in transferring pollen between flowers. Bees also make honey for their larvae to feed on. Other kinds of bee include mining bees, leaf-cutting bees; other kinds of wasp include ruby-tails, digger wasps, spider-hunters and mason wasps.

Spiders

Most people (including me) have an instinctive fear of spiders. There are some species, mainly in tropical countries, whose bite comes with a deadly *venom*. So there was good reason for our ancestors to be wary of these creatures. But fortunately in northern Europe no native species present any danger; there are a few potentially dangerous species in southern Europe, including the black widow.

Spiders have eight legs and usually as many eyes; the eyes are usually small and on top of the head. The hairs on their legs are very sensitive to vibration, so the spider can detect any movement nearby. They can often run very fast and usually feed on other insects. The largest spider in the world, the bird-eating spider of South America, is a hairy thing as big as a man's hand. You can guess what it eats!

◄ Spider – the large hind part is their abdomen or belly.

In wet and cold weather spiders often come into houses. It used to be said that, if you killed a spider, it would rain.

Spiders are the famous weavers or spinners (spin a thread) of the animal world. Many species build webs of fine thread-like nets in which to catch their prey. The commonest designs are the orb web, like a net stretched across an opening, and funnel-shaped webs. They also use their thread like a climbing rope to lower themselves and climb back up again.

Male spiders have to be very well-behaved when approaching a female; the females are usually much bigger than the males and sometimes kill them, if the male doesn't send the right signals.

The story goes like this: Long ago a lady known as Arachne (pronounced a-rack-knee) became famous for her weaving skill. But she was so famous that she became rather big-headed and boasted that she was better than the goddess

Athene. They quarrelled and when Arachne tried to kill herself, the goddess turned her into a spider. And that is why spiders are sometimes referred to as the daughters of Arachne. And this is how spiders got the name *arachnids* – daughters of Arachne.

▲ Spiders webs look beautiful in the frost or with the morning dew.

Other arachnids closely-related to spiders include harvestmen and scorpions. Harvestmen are like spiders but usually have a small round body and very long thin legs. Scorpions are lobster-like insects, with large claws. They also have a long tail ending in a sting; there are some scorpions in southern Europe whose sting is painful and dangerous to humans and some in the tropics that are very dangerous.

Other creepy-crawlies

▼ A male stag beetle – one of Europe's largest beetles.

Various other little monsters lurk underneath stones and logs, in cracks in walls and tree bark. Centipedes (the name means '100 feet', but they all have less than that) are swift predators pouncing on other insects with poison jaws. None in Britain are dangerous to humans, but further south there are some species to avoid. Millipedes are slower moving (with supposedly 1000 feet), feeding on plant matter; they sometimes curl up tightly, like a little spring, when disturbed.

Earwigs are scary looking scavengers, mostly active at night and hiding in cracks and under stones by day. But their rear pincers are weak and harmless, as are the large front antler-like pincers of stag beetles. They are the largest beetles in Britain and like to use old trees for their larvae.

Earwigs, centipedes and millipedes are widespread in many habitats and common in gardens. Wood lice are very common around houses as well as woods.

Bug zoo

You could quite easily set up a kind of zoo for these bugs in your garden or back yard. You just need to put out potential homes of various kinds and see what turns up. Lay out a log or small plank of wood, some rocks and a few upturned plant pots. You could scatter some straw or dead grasses and twigs around for a little more cover. Every morning take a look under some of the items to see what's there.

Try to lift logs and stones in one motion, without rocking them, and put them back gently so as not to harm anything.

Common garden insects include ladybirds and their larvae, bluebottles, hoverflies, midges, mosquitoes, lacewings, froghoppers, ground beetles, bumble bees, crab spiders and devil's coach-horses.

Slugs and snails

Solid slimy muscle, these primitive creatures are referred to as '*molluscs*' by scientists. This group also includes octopuses and squids. They have flexible bodies with no backbone and come out into the open mainly at night, spending the day sleeping in some hidden place, under a stone or in a crack somewhere. They are sensitive to loss of water and prefer moist conditions.

Slugs, and particularly snails with their extra protection, are found throughout the world both on land and in the sea. They eat mainly plants and can be a real pest to gardeners and farmers, eating into the best vegetable leaves. Slugs taste nasty to many predators and snails grow a shell for protection. The slime on slugs' bodies is a very sticky stuff, difficult to wash off hands or clothes. So it is best to pick them up with a short pair of twigs.

Snail tracks

Links

how predators
deal with snails,
see defences
p.36

▶ Battered snail
shells – a sign that
a predator has
eaten the snails.

▼ Song thrush – a
snail hunter.

You can often see where slugs and snails have been, by the tracks of dried slime they leave behind. The slime helps their 'foot' to grip surfaces. The best time to look for them is first thing in the morning when they are still fresh. You could lay a piece of black card over a regular trail, if you want to get a close-up of a genuine slime track.

If you have the larger garden snails around your garden, you could try marking their shells. If you put numbers on them, you could keep track of their movements. Use enamel paint with a fine brush and make sure you don't get any paint on the snail's body – this will harm it.

Broken snail shells in the garden by a rock are usually a sign that something has been eating the snails – probably a song thrush.

Things to look for

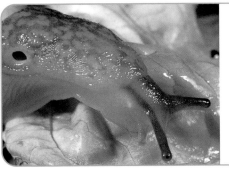

Get a magnifying glass and take a close look at a snail's or a slug's eyes. Approach it very carefully so as not to frighten it. They are very slow movers and when they feel threatened, snails retract into their shells and slugs shrink their bodies. They also withdraw their tentacles, which have their eyes and smelling organs on the ends.

Fish

Stickleback, minnow, loach, bullhead, gudgeon, eel, trout, salmon, pike, dace, roach, perch, carp, tench, bream, herring, mackerel, flatfish, gurnard, sprat, cod, haddock, bass, mullet, wrasse, ray, skate, shark.

Backbones

Fish were the first animals to develop backbones. In fact, if you examine the skeleton of most kinds of fish there is little else other than the skull and backbone – all the rib-bones run from the backbone and are really quite thin. Backbones are a very efficient way of providing a flexible structure to the softer parts of the body and enabling animals to have larger bodies. Fish are the ancestors of amphibians who became the first *vertebrates* on dry land.

The largest fish in the world is the whale shark, which grows to about 15m in length, and feeds on plankton, so is not aggressive to humans. The largest fish in northern Europe is the basking shark; again this is a plankton feeder and harmless to humans.

▼ Eels sometimes wriggle over land, looking for a pond or river.

Fish are the largest freshwater animals in our region. The largest sea creatures are the whales but, along with dolphins, although they look like fish, they are actually mammals. This is something very interesting, that scientists call *convergent evolution*, where unrelated animals end up looking very similar, because they live in similar ways. In the case of whales and fish, an elongated shape with fins and a sail-like tail has proved a successful shape for swimming in water.

Fish have all sorts of shapes: long and thin, like eels; squashed flat, like flatfish and rays; very narrow like bream, but all tend to be longer than they are wide. Rudder-like fins give fish extra control in moving through water.

Fish are able to extract oxygen from water through their gills, but mammals need to return to the surface to breathe. Most fish are either freshwater fish, living in rivers and lakes, or saltwater fish living in the sea; but some, like salmon, live part of their lives in each.

Salmon – a migratory fish

Salmon lay their eggs in streams and when the young hatch out, they continue to live in the stream for their first few years. Then as they grow, they follow the river to the sea, where they feed well and grow quickly. After another year or two, when fully grown, they return and travel up the same river they were born in, to breed. They can leap waterfalls up to about 2m high on their way up a river. There are some good places to watch this in the autumn, though there are not as many salmon returning as there used to be. Pollution and over-fishing has reduced their numbers.

If you live near one of the northern coast rivers where salmon run, try to find out if there are any regular 'leaps' – waterfalls where salmon can be seen jumping. October is the best month, particularly after a spell of rain.

▼ An autumn spectacle.

Nature Safari

What might you see?

OK, what might you find in a nearby pond or stream? Well, depending on what region you are in, the small fish in the edge may be sticklebacks or minnows and the slightly larger fish in more open water could be dace or trout.

Trout have spotted sides and usually swim at mid-depth, rising to the surface to take items of food. Dace are silvery fish of about 15 to 20cm length, that patrol the surface of streams; this is why they sometimes get called skimmers. Sticklebacks are more solitary and territorial, move in a hover-and-dart way and prefer still or slow-moving water. Minnows tend to move continuously, live in *shoals* and prefer flowing water.

▲ Male stickleback.

You may be lucky and spot a large torpedo shape hovering in mid-water near the edge, just its fins flickering to maintain its position. Pike are fierce-looking predators, that make sudden lunges to catch other fish that swim near. And often that is all you'll see of them – a sudden swirl in the side of the pool, as the fish propels itself away to safety at your approach. They are dark with lovely green patterns on the side (well-camouflaged) and can grow to over 1m long.

▼ A young salmon –very similar to a trout.

There are stories of monster pike attacking dogs that have waded into the water's edge of a lake, but such events are very rare. There are even stories of pike attacking people, but I am not sure that any have proved to be true!

There is a wider variety of fish species in the sea, some of which can be hard to identify. Watch out for flatfish on sandy beaches and blennies in rockpools. To see what kind of fish are living further out to sea, you could visit a harbour or quayside fish market, when the fishing boats are returning.

Catching tiddlers

Let's try catching some of the small fish – tiddlers – and take a close look at them. Get a fishing net at the end of a long stick and find a place where you can reach some fish without having to stretch so far that you might fall in. It is no good trying to swish your net after the fish. Even the smallest fish can swim faster than you can move your net through the water: fish are *stream-lined* to slip through water easily, but a net is broad and offers a lot of resistance to the water.

You need to move the opening of your net very, very slowly towards the fish – preferably towards the fish's head – and under. When you have got the fish in the opening of the net, quickly and suddenly sweep it up. If the fish escapes, take your time and try again as the fish settle down after the disturbance to their world.

If you have a little silvery fish wriggling in your net, you need to get it back into water as soon as you can. If you haven't got a jar of water to put the fish in and have a good look at it, a plastic bag might do – provided there are no holes in it. Alternatively you could make a little pool in the gravel or sand at the water's edge, that you can put your catch into.

Ideally you should empty the fish from the net straight into your container; if you do have to handle it, be very gentle. Then when you have seen enough, remember to let all your fish go, otherwise they might die. Minnows are particularly hard to look after, since they need plenty of fresh water (with lots of oxygen to breath).

Be careful with sticklebacks, as they have sharp spines on their back and sides, which are not always obvious since they only raise them when frightened. If you have a fish tank at home, you may be able to keep some sticklebacks for a while, provided you look after them. Then you will notice some interesting things about these fish. The males become brilliantly-coloured and aggressive in the spring and each builds a nest to invite females to breed with him.

Fishing with a net for these small fish is a good way to learn about fish behaviour. Then you'll be well prepared for the next step – fishing with a rod and line.

Links

ponds and rivers
p.120
harbours p.118

Not really fish

Whales and dolphins are not common in the seas of Europe, but there are some places where they are seen regularly. You usually have to go out in a boat to see them, because, as large creatures, they prefer to stay in deeper water. Sometimes they allow boats to approach very close and dolphins will occasionally swim alongside the boat. They have a smaller relative, the porpoise, that looks very similar, and these are seen from the shore much more often, in harbours, estuaries or sea inlets.

Plants

Trees, bushes, shrubs, herbs, flowers, grasses, reeds, sedges, mosses, ferns, seaweeds

▲ Orchids are always worth a close look.

► Fern – a plant that doesn't flower.

Links

trees and photosynthesis, woodlands p.98

trees and photosynthesis, woodlands p.98

► Horsetails are an ancient plant, related to ferns, common in damp areas. Their ancestors grew to the height of trees and formed forests before the era of the dinosaurs.

Plants cover the earth in a green blanket that absorbs energy from the sun in the process known as *photosynthesis*. Fungi are classed separately from plants since they feed only on decaying matter, not sunlight. The most numerous group of plants produce elaborate flower heads; mosses and ferns are more ancient and non-flowering. Look on the underside of fern leaves to see their seeds or 'spores'.

Flowering plants evolved about 100 million years ago, relatively recently in the history of plants. Some, like grasses and deciduous trees, do not produce obvious flowers. Different species of plant flower at different times of the year, but spring and summer are the main seasons. Make a note of which plant's flowers attract the most insects. When pollen is passed between flowers, usually by insects, fertile seed heads can develop; some seed heads become berries and fruit.

Plants compete for the sun's light and the tallest wins. That is why trees eventually colonise any land that is left alone. Over time, weeds and grasses colonise bare ground, then come bushes and finally trees.

Nature Safari

Some common wild flowers

Daisy, buttercup, primrose, dandelion, herb robert, wild rose, willowherb, clover, foxglove, red campion, forget-me-not

Good places for wild flowers

Hedgerows, riversides, meadows, woodland edges, sand dunes

◄ Meadow cranesbill – a common roadside flower in summer.

Dandelions

From a gardener's point of view, dandelions are weeds. But that only means they are a wild invader of his planned flower bed. However, they produce beautiful flowers all through spring and summer, attractive to many insects and the leaves are good to eat. Good for tortoises and rabbits and for people in salads.

▶ The dandelion's flower turns into a ball of seeds. It is said that you can tell the time by the number of blows it takes to blow all the seeds off the stems.

Nettles

Links

wildlife
gardening p.92

Nettles are the front-line troops of the plant world; they invade waste ground and keep people out. Their weapon is their sting. The hairs on the leaves contain formic acid, which causes irritation and a burning sensation when the ends of the hairs break on our skin. Try soothing the sting with dock leaves.

Nettles are the preferred food plant for the caterpillars of several species of butterfly; small tortoiseshells and peacock butterflies are frequently seen around nettles. But believe it or not, they are also an excellent food plant for us humans and in the past were eaten more often, in soups, boiled as green vegetables and to make a tea-like drink. They are rich in several vitamins and iron (which our bodies need in small quantities).

Sundew and butterwort – carnivorous plants

▲ Sundew catch small insects with their sticky bristles.

These plants tend to grow on acid soils, low in nutrients. But they have a deadly secret for getting these essential foods: they trap small insects on their sticky leaves. The leaves produce digestive juices and the insect is dissolved and absorbed. They also 'eat' pollen and particles of other plants in this way when they are blown onto the leaves. Butterwort leaves look harmless enough, but sundew leaves are more sinister-looking, like green paws ringed with sticky red hairs. Why not try a drawing of this plant feeding?

Some berries are very poisonous to humans; never eat berries unless an adult has said they are OK. Also be aware the stem and leaves of some plants, such as hemlock, are poisonous.

projects

make a daisy chain

Pick some daisies. Make a short split in the stem of one and thread the stem of another through the split. Make a split in that stem then thread another through the split. And so on. To round the chain, you will have to thread the flower carefully through the last stem.

Growing plants from seeds

You can grow some really nice plants from fruit seeds, although they won't produce fruit.
You can use seeds from apples, oranges, lemons, peaches, dates. Soak the seeds overnight in water then plant in small pots (yoghurt pots are good) filled with soil. Keep in a warm, dark place for a few weeks. When shoots appear, place the pots on a sunny windowsill and water the plants if the soil feels dry.

Growing coloured flowers

A good way to see how the stem of a plant works is to colour flowers or celery.
You will need:
White flower or stick of celery
A jar of water
Coloured ink/paint

1. Put the ink/paint into the jar to colour the water.
2. Stand the flower or celery in the jar.
3. After a while, you will see the flower or celery change colour as the water is drawn up the stem.
4. If you have used celery, cut through it and you will see coloured dots. These are the tubes the water passes through to get to the leaves.

Four-leaf clover

Most clover leaves are in groups of three on a stem. Occasionally there are four, and very rarely five. It is said to bring luck, when you find a four-leaf clover.

Mushrooms and toadstools

▲ Fly agaric – a classic toadstool and very poisonous.

Mushrooms and toadstools are strange plant-like growths that can appear quite suddenly where yesterday there was no sign of them. They belong to a group called fungi (the plural of fungus), related to plants. Other kinds of fungi include moulds and mildew.

Fungi lack chlorophyll – the substance which gives plants their green colour and enables them to use sunlight. They generally feed on decaying matter in the soil or in the wood of trees, but some kinds can also grow on living plants and animals (yuck!).

▲ Fungi also grow on trees.

The mushroom or toadstool that we see growing is only a small part of a fungus: it is like the flower of a plant, produced to generate seeds. The main body of a fungus is a network of fine threads within the soil or wood it is feeding on. The seeds of a fungus aren't like the seeds of other plants, they are a very fine powder called spores.

If you've ever stepped on a dry puff-ball and seen the smoke-like dust explode out of it, then you've seen the spores of a fungus. Try it. And don't worry – you're not destroying the fungus; you're helping it to spread and generate new plants.

Another way of seeing the spores of a fungus is to pick a mushroom and leave the head on a clean sheet of paper overnight, with the gills facing down.

Fungi play an important part in their communities, by breaking down waste matter and dead things. They release nutrients to the soil, which then become available to other plants.

▶ Parasol mushroom – the cap can grow to 25cms across.

Nature Safari

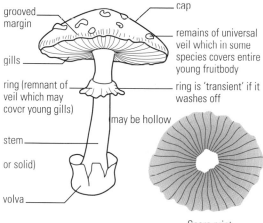

grooved margin

cap

remains of universal veil which in some species covers entire young fruitbody

gills

ring (remnant of veil which may cover young gills)

ring is 'transient' if it washes off

may be hollow

stem

or solid)

volva

Spore print

Links

'fungal forays', see special events p.186 recycling energy p.31

Closely related to fungi are the lichens. These grow on rocks and trees like crusts, forming strange and beautiful patterns. They are slow-growing and sensitive to air pollution, so are usually a sign of the age of whatever they are growing on and the clean air around. They are the first colonisers of bare rock.

▼ Different lichen species often grow together to form colourful patterns.

project

grow your own fungus

You don't need any seeds to grow a fungus – their spores are actually in the air around us. Leave a piece of fruit or a slice of bread in a warm place for a few days and you'll see moulds begin to grow on it.

Safety

There are a number of toadstools and other fungi that are very, very poisonous. And the dangerous thing is that they can be very difficult to recognise; in fact one of the deadliest, the destroying angel, is similar to the edible field mushroom. It is best not to touch any toadstool you're unsure of, just in case. And only take the advice of a reliable expert for identifying species.

▼ Edible or poisonous? Sometimes they can be very difficult to tell apart.

Check your surroundings:

habitats and their communities

Gardens and parks

Although they may turn up in some unusual places, plants and animals do not live just anywhere: every species has its own preferences. The kind of place a species tends to live in, is called its habitat. Various species of both plants and animals have similar preferences and tend to be found together in the same places. Ecologists call such groups, and their habitats, 'communities'.

Within communities, especially old-established ones, the lives of different creatures are often connected in unusual ways. Large blue butterflies can live on chalk grasslands happily as adults, but for the species to survive they need another member of the community to be there as well. As caterpillars they need ants: the caterpillar feeds on the ant larvae and in return produces a juice that the ants feed on. They are quite rare because they have such specialised requirements.

Gardens and parks are often in built-up areas and can be quite busy with people, but they also provide a good home and a living for many kinds of wild creature. Not so much the big beasts – though some ancient parks have herds of deer – but various kinds of bird, squirrels, foxes, frogs, toads and some specialised insects can all thrive in these human spaces. Bigger wild animals tend to be more wary and need larger, undisturbed areas for *territories*.

▼ Mandarin duck are often seen on park ponds.

There is one great bonus to watching animals in parks and gardens: they are used to having people around and, because of this, are much less timid. You can approach some animals and birds closely. You may be able to feed grey squirrels or house sparrows from your hand in a park. If there is a pond or lake, there may be some unusual or wild ducks there.

Nature Safari

You can get close enough to check out the pochard's deep red eye or the tufted duck's golden eye.

The other benefits to watching wildlife in your garden or somewhere close to your home is that you can visit it regularly, get to know the place well and see it through the changing seasons.

A kind of forest

Think about the parks and gardens you know – what are they made up of? What is their natural character? They are usually a patchwork of short grass lawns, longer grasses and flowers, bushes and trees; and possibly a pond of some size and even occasionally a stream. This is very like the edge or a clearing of a natural forest, one of the richest habitat types for wildlife. Stone or brick houses and concrete or gravel are just like rock outcrops or dry sandy areas.

The kinds of animal that might visit any particular garden or park depend on the surroundings. If there are plenty of trees or a wood close-by and good ground cover, then more species are likely to visit. But roads act as barriers for animals that cannot fly.

Hedgehogs, badgers and reptiles only tend to visit gardens or live in parks, where they border onto open countryside. Insects and birds are more mobile because they can fly, so they can turn up wherever there is a suitable habitat.

TIP • TIP • TIP • TIP • TIP • TIP • TIP • TIP

- In built-up areas of towns keep an eye out for the disused bits of land: these are often places of refuge for wildlife. Places that have good wildlife potential include the ground alongside railway tracks (you can look from bridges or paths running alongside), church yards (including lichens on gravestones), canals and rivers.
- Some animals, like foxes, crows and magpies, have learnt to scavenge on our left-overs. Discarded take-aways and rubbish bins with the remains of food provide good and regular pickings for them.
- If houses have eaves, it is always worth casting a glance up at them. Swifts, swallows and house martins all nest under the eaves of houses. Eaves are where the roofing of a house sticks out beyond the walls.

Feeding animals

Links

feeding birds
p.97

You can attract birds and other animals to a garden or elsewhere by putting out food for them. Think about where you put the food and where the animal might feel secure eating it. Then you will have to wait for the local wildlife to discover your food source. It is much better if you can do this on a regular basis – better for the animals themselves and better for attracting them for viewing.

If hedgehogs or foxes visit your garden, you can put out left-over scraps of meat, or a little pet food. Nuts and seeds are good for birds. Blackbirds and other thrushes will be pleased with any rotten apples during the winter. Mice and voles may also be attracted to fruit. You can paint a sugary s olution on a fence or tree trunk for moths. Clear up old scraps from your feeding area every now and then, so as not to encourage rats.

Links

approaching wild
creatures p.143

Be aware – wild animals sometimes bite, usually only when they are frightened or threatened. Occasionally, a nervous creature feeding from your hand gets startled by a sudden movement and gives you a nip; or sometimes it is an accidental nibble as they take the food from your hand. Always be wary when a strange dog approaches, particularly on mainland Europe where some dogs and wild mammals carry rabies, a serious disease.

Parks: when and where?

Try a deer park in the month of October. Leaves will be starting to die back and colours turning from green to golden brown. Red deer stags and fallow bucks (the males) begin 'rutting': it is the mating season and the males display, challenging each other with deep bellowing sounds, and just occasionally fighting. Within 10km of the centre of London you can witness red deer stags go through their ancient ritual in Richmond Park. Treat them with respect though and do not approach too closely.

Nature Safari

It is also the conker season. Conkers are the seeds or nuts of the horse chestnut tree – nuts that some animals can eat, but not people. The gorgeously-polished nut of the ripe fruit falls from the tree at this time, in its padded, spiky casing, which often splits as it hits the ground to reveal the nut. Collect a few of the biggest ones to play conkers with.

▲ Conkers have soft outer shells that protect them when they fall to the ground.

Conkers

Get an adult to push a hole through the middle of the conker with a nail or thin screwdriver. Get a piece of string about 30cms long and tie a knot in one end. Thread this through the conker so it sits on the knot. You then take turns with an opponent to swing your conker at the other until one breaks up. The survivor is the winner – and conqueror.

Wildlife gardening

It is really quite easy to make any garden friendly to wildlife – you just have to do nothing. Just imagine if you could do your homework by doing nothing, just sitting and watching your garden grow. Actually in a few years your patch (we can't really call it a garden now) would perhaps become a bit of a jungle, with high nettles and other weeds, with probably a tree or two sprouting. Friendly to all sorts of insects and other creepy-crawlies, but not so good for us humans.

So, whereas most gardeners like to keep their garden very tidy and looking pretty and neatly organised, some overgrown areas and certain weeds would help to provide more homes for wildlife.

Good flowers for wildlife

Dandelion, knapweed, foxglove, teasel, buttercup, yarrow, honeysuckle, bramble, ox-eye daisy, lady's bedstraw, lady's smock

Nettles are the main food plant of several widespread butterflies: small tortoiseshells, peacock butterflies and painted ladies. Meadow browns might visit your patch of meadow; these were very common butterflies over a wide area until quite recently, but are now only in favoured places like flower meadows and damp grassland. Hoverflies should arrive and patrol the area around the brambles.

▶ Small tortoiseshell butterfly on nettles.

If your garden is big enough, a patch of nettles and brambles would be excellent. Nettles should move in quite soon if you neglect an area; brambles might need some help. Then around that area, you could scatter a border of wild meadow flowers (you should be able to find a packet of seeds in a local gardening centre). This mixture of plants will provide a home and feeding for quite a wide range of flying insects including bees, hoverflies, butterflies and moths.

It will help if you can choose an area facing south or south east (to catch the sun) and maybe sheltered by trees or shrubs to the west or north (from the winds). The directions might be different depending on the shape of the land around your garden or how near the sea is.

A few logs lying on the ground provide homes for those creepy-crawlies that like to live their lives hidden from the open air, such as centipedes and millipedes, beetles and wood lice. There's an impressive spider with large fangs that preys on wood lice. It has no English name, but is quite common in gardens.

▼ Wood louse – a common garden crustacean, sometimes known as a 'slater'.

Other features you might consider to increase the diversity in your garden: a compost heap, a pile of sticks, branches or logs, some shrubs that have berries in the autumn, a honeysuckle trellis, maybe even a small dry underground chamber.

If you have a little more space, and want to attract even more butterflies – plant a buddleia bush. This is sometimes called the 'butterfly bush', for the obvious reason that its flowers seem to be irresistible to a wide range of butterflies. Another plant with similar attraction to butterflies, but not so big, is hemp agrimony.

Once the insects move in, then you've created further links in the food chain; with a bit of luck some other types of bird will visit your garden and maybe even nest in your wild area.

▼ Earwig – it's pincers are harmless.

If you live in the city or somewhere with a really small garden, the best thing is to try to vary the area that you do have and create some cover for free-living things – places they can hide among leaves or under stones. Then see what turns up. If you have no garden at all – you'll have to persuade an adult to take you to the park, or set up an environment for a pet. Small fish can be made quite at home. But any animal kept as a pet needs to be looked after every day. You control their world, so make sure they have a world in which they can live healthily and contentedly.

Things to look out for in your garden

Under logs, rocks or suchlike: *wood lice, centipedes, spiders, beetles, slugs*
Among plants: *spiders and their webs, flies, butterflies, moths, caterpillars, ladybirds*
In bushes and trees: *birds, squirrels, insects*
Pond and damp area: *frogs, toads, dragonflies, snails, pond insects*
At dusk: *bats, moths*

project

dig a pond

If you want a challenge that will really boost the wildlife in a garden, create a pond. You will need to buy a sheet of material to line the bed of the pond and hold in the water. This can be quite expensive, so it may be a project to do through your school.

You will also need a few plants to get the pond environment started; then you could add some frog spawn in the spring.

The more natural you can make the edges, the better it is for wildlife. It is good to have some sort of island, even a stone or a log sticking out above the water. There are many things you can do to add wildlife interest to a pond, so it would be worth asking for some advice (try one of the organisations listed at the back of this book) or doing some research in a more detailed book.

▲ Common frogs find their way to most ponds.

Links

growing from seeds p.83
frog spawn p.57
catching insects p.60

Garden birds

Almost all gardens, even window boxes or small back yards in the middle of cities, get visited by birds sometimes. It could be a pigeon, a house sparrow or a blue tit, or occasionally something rarer. If you live in a high-rise flat in the city you may be able to get good views from your windows of a kestrel hovering. They regularly nest on the window ledges of tall buildings, but you would have to be very lucky for a pair to nest on your window ledge, since they have plenty of choice in most areas.

▲ The acrobatic great tit and blue tit are regular visitors to peanut feeders.

It is quite easy to attract more birds to your garden and increase the number of species – just provide them with some food. You can also put up a nest box and see if you can tempt a pair to breed.

Blue tits and great tits take readily to nest boxes, since they usually nest in holes in trees or walls, so a nest box suitable for these species would be a good one to start with. Put it in a quieter part of the garden (i.e. not right next to a busy door); if you can see it from one of your windows, then you will be able to watch what goes on. It would be best at least 1m from the ground, in a position that would be hard for cats (or rats!) to climb to.

Although many resident birds (including blue and great tits) may not nest until the spring, round about April time, they are looking at potential nest sites and maybe doing some nest building through the late winter, in February and March. So you need to get your nest box up by the time snowdrops are flowering.

If you learn to identify the birds in your garden, your help would be welcome for one of the garden bird surveys that get organised each year. You just need to make a note of what visits your garden on a certain day. (If you want to take your interest further, get in touch with the RSPB – see p.187.)

Feeding birds

Think about where to put your feeders: somewhere where the birds will feel secure, with cover nearby, but where you can get a good view from one of your house windows. Or you could put out two feeders. One well down the garden to attract and encourage birds into the garden; and one near the window to get close looks at the bolder species. Try to identify which species are visiting your feeders.

The two main foods to put out are nuts and a seed mix. Peanuts (unsalted!) are best put in a hanging feeder; you can get special hanging feeders for seeds too, or you can put seeds on a bird table, a raised platform or simply scatter them on the ground. Old apples are good for blackbirds and thrushes during cold spells; you may be lucky and find some of the Scandinavian thrushes, fieldfares and redwings, have joined them. They all seem to prefer rotten apples to fresh ones.

If there is no pond nearby, you could put out some water for the birds to drink and bathe in. Seed-eating birds in particular get very thirsty.

Sometimes you may find some unexpected visitors to your feeder

▲ The nuthatch is a specialist at going down trees.

◀ Goldfinches like seeds

The commonest garden birds in the UK

1. Starling
2. House Sparrow
3. Blue Tit
4. Blackbird
5. Chaffinch
6. Greenfinch
7. Collared Dove
8. Great Tit
9. Woodpigeon
10. Robin

Other birds you might see in your garden: pied wagtail, song thrush, wren, dunnock, swallow, house martin, coal tit, goldfinch, siskin, black-headed gull, magpie, carrion crow, sparrowhawk.

Forests

The Earth's forests are the natural power station of the planet; they harness the sun's energy in a process known as *photosynthesis*. Green plants all capture the sun's energy directly through this process, but in a forest community this happens on a large scale.

With the help of sunlight, plant leaves take in the carbon dioxide in the Earth's atmosphere. Carbon dioxide is made up of carbon and oxygen, both of which are essential ingredients in animal life. The plants absorb the carbon and put out the oxygen. We use oxygen through our breathing and carbon – well, carbon is something of a magic element. No, it doesn't do party tricks, but it combines in many different ways with other elements and is the building block of all life. As well as providing the main material for the bodies of plants and animals, it's also the basic element in oil, coal and even diamonds.

So, the chain goes like this: green plants – photosynthesis – carbon and oxygen – sources of energy – animal life. The reason conservationists worry about too much tree-felling and the loss of the world's forests, because plants play such an essential part in the energy cycle of our planet.

Forests also create a sheltered environment for other species to inhabit. The trees break the force of the wind and the fall of rain. They provide cool shade from the heat of the summer sun, which is worth remembering on a hot summer's day. Light and shade create the essence of woods.

▼ You can find trees of all ages in a forest. This tree is hundreds of years old.

Do you know how to work out your direction in a forest? Well, moss usually grows better on the north side of a tree, since it tends to dry out on the south side, where the sun can shine on it directly. Many kinds of mosses and fungi thrive in moist sheltered places and old woods should have a rich collection of different kinds of plant and animal.

Nature Safari

Forests

Woodlands

Woodlands are our own version of the jungles of tropical regions. Most are not quite so overgrown nor as rich in animal life as true jungles, since they have been managed by us humans for years or, even centuries. But if we left them alone for a long time, our woods and fields would return to an overgrown tangle more like a jungle – the ancient 'Wildwood'.

For thousands of years northern Europe was gripped in an ice age and the ground was frozen or covered in ice sheets. This was too harsh for most plants to grow; just a few tough heathers, tussock grasses and short flowers hung on around the southern edge of the frozen lands, like the Arctic today. This kind of landscape is known as tundra.

▲ There were no trees in Britain and northern Europe during the ice ages, which ended 10,000 years ago.

Then around 10,000 years ago the climate warmed and thawed out the lands, gradually pushing the frozen zone further north. Pioneering plants and trees spread from the south. First juniper, birch and pine, then broad-leaved trees like oak, ash and alder. Wait a minute though – plants cannot move, they are rooted to the ground. So how did they spread? The answer is in their seeds.

Seeds

All plants, including trees, have evolved cunning ways of getting their seeds to travel and thus spread their species. Some wrap their seeds in a tasty fruit – food for an animal. The seed passes through the animal, protected by its outer husk, and is dropped somewhere along the way, far from its parent bush, in a small pile of 'fertiliser'. Best not go into that! Other plants, like dandelions, use the wind: they have fluffy seeds that can float away down the wind to start a new life. Some trees have winged seeds, others produce nuts.

Sycamore fruits have a twisted wing like a propeller blade. Instead of dropping straight to the earth, spinning slows its fall and it rides any breeze that's blowing. Autumn and early winter are good times to find sycamore helicopters: throw one up in the air and it should spin to earth – a light breeze helps.

▼ Young ash seeds and leaves in spring.

▼ Ripe sycamore seeds in autumn.

project

make a helicopter seed

Some seeds spin like helicopter blades as they fall to the ground.

To make your own you will need:
Thin card
Paper clip or blu-tac
Scissors

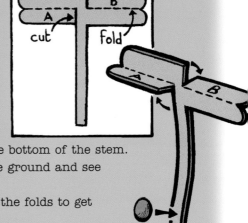

1. Cut a shape as shown out of card.
2. Cut along the dotted lines.
3. Fold up along line A and down along line B.
4. Put the paper clip or blu-tac on the bottom of the stem.
5. Hold your helicopter high from the ground and see it spin to the ground.
6. You may need to experiment with the folds to get it to fly properly.

Links

growing from seeds p.83

Things to look (and listen) for in woodlands

Woodpeckers, squirrels, deer, signs of badgers and foxes, bats in the evening, owls at night, leaf shapes, bark patterns, the fruits of trees, birdsong in spring, the cooing of woodpigeons in summer, butterflies in summer, wood ant nests, fungi in autumn, large fungi growing on trees, beetles under logs and on tree trunks, woodpecker nest holes, insect holes, the tunnelling patterns of bark beetle larvae

How to recognise an ancient wood

In lowland areas an ancient wood is likely to have tall trees; in northern, exposed areas there are ancient woods with short, gnarled trees, where the rough weather stunts their growth. Mosses, lichens and ferns actually growing on the tree trunks and branches are a good sign, especially lichens, since they are slow to colonise and grow. There's likely to be some very old trees with deeply-cracked bark. If it's an undisturbed wood, there should be some fallen tree trunks around, rotting into the earth, often covered in moss and sprouting fungi.

Links

mushrooms and
toadstools p.84

◀ Club fungus and mosses growing on rotting wood.

▼ Wood anemone.

But the best indicators are particular species of lichens, fungi, plants and insects that only seem to be able to survive in a full old woodland community. Ancient woodland flowers include wood anemone, bluebells, dog's mercury, solomon's seal, enchanter's night shade. Some wild flowers certainly have poetic names.

Trees

Trees are the largest plants on earth. In fact the largest living things and the longest-lived. There are living trees that are thought to be 2000 years old. The tallest trees are the giant redwoods of North America that grow to 100m high. A tree needs a large root system to grow to this height; the roots absorb nutrients and water from the soil and they also hold the tree upright.

The tough outer skin, the tree's bark, gives the inner wood some protection; it grows rougher with age and its crevices offer good hiding places for insects and spiders. You can learn to recognise different types of tree from the patterns of their bark.

The various kinds of oak are the most numerous and widespread trees in Europe. Their leaves have a wavy edge. Oaks support many different types of insect, so birds feed well in summer oakwoods. Oaks are also the tree that the ancient druids held sacred.

Without the farming activities of people, trees would cover much larger areas of land than they do. But for thousands of years humans have been clearing away areas of ancient wood to create fields for farm animals and for growing crops. Though there are many new plantations, there are now very few areas of original forest left on the earth.

▼ Acorns are the nut of the oak tree and provide food for many birds and mammals.

When trees grow together forming a wood, they create their own, more sheltered environment. On a windy day it will be calmer inside a wood since the trees absorb the force of the wind. In cold, frosty weather it's usually just a little bit warmer in the wood – maybe just above freezing – and that can be a matter of life or death for many plants and animals. Likewise on a hot, dry day in summer, it is cooler in the shade of a wood and more moist.

Leaves

Trees can be divided into two groups: deciduous trees are those which grow a new covering of leaves each year and evergreens are trees that keep their leaves all year long. Deciduous trees include beech, elm, lime, ash and some oak species. Most conifers, yew and holly are evergreens. Conifers, like pine, fir and spruce, all have thin needle-like leaves. Take a look at some pine needles under a microscope and you should be able to see the small holes they breathe through.

Different kinds of tree have different shaped leaves, but all leaves have a system of veins that provide a frame for the leaf and bring water. Leaves of deciduous trees turn to many different colours, yellows, golds and reds, when they die in the autumn.

▲ Pine – its leaves are like needles and its seeds grow protected in woody cones.

◄ Oak leaf

Investigating trees

What lives in a tree?

You can find out what is living in a tree by shaking the branches gently and catching things as they fall out. Get friends to hold an old white sheet or pillowcase under the branch as you shake. Try using firm white card if you have no-one to help you; or ideally the lid of a box, which has a rim, such as a shoe box. This slows any agile bugs from escaping.

Tree art

▲ Bark of the ash tree.

Bark rubbings

Bark on trees varies a lot and when old bark cracks it forms some attractive patterns. You can record these patterns by 'bark rubbing'. Fix some thick paper to the tree trunk with tape. Rub firmly over the paper with a crayon – do the patterns vary from tree to tree?

Leaf rubbing

You can also make patterns with leaves. Place the leaf upside down and lay some paper over it. Rub over the paper gently with a soft pencil – the veins of the leaf become clear. Try a gold or silver crayon on dark paper.

Leaf pressing

You can keep a record of leaves you have seen by pressing them in a book. You can use your diary, but a book with absorbent paper is ideal. Place the leaves inside the book, leaving enough room around them to label them. Close the book and place a large stone or weight on top of the book, which will flatten the leaves.

How old is it?

When a tree is felled and you can see a cross-section of its trunk, you can get a close estimate of its age by counting the rings. The number of rings is the age of the tree in years. A tree's growth is dependent on the seasons, varying from slow in the winter cold, to swift in the summer sunshine. So each year leaves its mark in the core growth of the tree.

How to identify trees

Tree species can be identified by a mixture of three things: the shape of their leaves, the pattern of their bark and the shape of the whole tree.

Links

seasons p.172
plants p.80

◄◄◄ Leaves from an oak tree.

◄◄ Leaves from a beech tree.

◄ Leaves from an ash tree.

Diary projects

Go out and collect examples of three obviously different kinds of leaves. Take your time to grasp their differences, then in your diary (or a sheet of paper if you don't have a diary) draw or paint each leaf – leaving a space beneath it for some writing. Now find a tree identification book in the library or look on the internet, and work out which trees' leaves you have. Write their names beneath your drawing of their leaves.

Do you have a tree outside your house? In the spring, take a look at it every day; when you see the first leaves open on the branches, make a note of the date in your diary. When the leaves are fully open, try to identify what kind of tree it is and add that to your diary. Next year do the same thing. Was the tree earlier or later coming into leaf? Write down in your diary why you think that might be.

By the sea

'Water, water everywhere and not a drop to drink'. Was the Ancient Mariner, who said this, mad? No, because he was at sea, with no fresh water. As you'll know if you've been swimming in the sea and accidentally taken a gulp of water, sea water is very salty and no good for drinking.

Oceans and seas cover two-thirds of our planet's surface and millions of different creatures have evolved to live in its waters. In fact, life is thought to have started in the sea. It may appear static, but is always in motion. Tides sweep up and down coasts. Waves and swells lap at the land. Heat from the sun causes ocean currents and the water of all rivers eventually flows into the sea.

The open sea and its depths don't reveal their secrets easily, but if you take a trip on a ferry or a short cruise in a good area you might see some of its creatures – sea-birds, seals and, if you're lucky, dolphins. As is often the

▼ Rocky coastline – where the sea eats away at the land.

Nature Safari

◀ Stormy waves
reveal the power
of the sea.

Links

special events
p.186

case, it's best to do a little research to find out the best places: all these creatures have traditional gathering places where people have been watching them for centuries. They sometimes move into new areas as well though, as conditions change over time.

▼ Killer whale – a
sea mammal.

Where land meets sea

The part of the sea that we are most familiar with is the edge strip where land and sea meet – the coast. Even above the high watermark, the shape of the land can be affected by the closeness of the sea: rocks and hard-packed soils may be eroded by storms into cliffs, or there may be sand dunes or a saltmarsh that occasionally gets flooded by sea water. And where better to go on a hot summer's day. Apart from swimming, jumping waves and building sandcastles, what's there to do?

Flotsam and jetsam

All things get washed up on the shore eventually; at least all floating and lighter objects that cannot resist the tides, currents and occasional storms. Sadly there is much human rubbish washed up on many beaches now, along with the seaweed, shells and other stuff. Try doing a careful search of a beach and see what you can find. This is known as beach-combing.

▼ Even remote beaches get all sorts of things washed up on the shore.

Most of what the sea throws up is left along the high tide line – often called just the tide-line or strand-line. As you might expect, this is at the upper part of a beach. Sometimes large or unusual animals and fish get

washed up on the shore. Maybe a large turtle that has drifted up from more tropical waters further south. Or a dead whale. Many people find such strandings interesting to visit (though usually a bit smelly!). They provide a connection with distant exotic places and the mystery of the sea.

Nature Safari

On the beach

Sand or shingle? Shingle is generally harder to walk on – though soft sand can be hard work too. There is probably more wildlife on sandy beaches, but there are a number of more specialised creatures that can be seen on shingle beaches, such as little terns, various plovers, certain plants like sea holly, and some rare bush-crickets.

Not too many wild creatures live in or on open sand, unless there is vegetable material (live or dead) around. Sometimes sandhoppers can be teeming in their thousands around old seaweed and under bits of wood. They're like a cross between a shrimp and a wood louse. Little worm-like piles of sand are a sign there's a lugworm beneath the surface. Living cockle-shells and razor-shells lie buried in some sands. There may be a scattering of wading birds or gulls along the water's edge. Look out for the oystercatcher – black and white with a long red beak.

▲ Sandhopper – like a large flea, but harmless.

◀ Oystercatchers probe the sand looking for shellfish.

TIP • TIP

When the wind is
blowing on the beach,
you are better off
looking for a hollow in
the dunes (if there are
some), where you can
enjoy the day sheltered
from the wind.

You may find a few fish in the water over gently-sloping sand or in tidal pools. A face-mask and snorkel helps to see them; but you should be a good swimmer and have an adult with you before you try it in the sea. You might see sand-eels, small flatfish such as flounders, herring and mackerel fry (young fish).

Water over sand near rocks often has more fish, but you need to be careful that the sea's swell doesn't push you onto the rocks.

Keep an eye out for terns fishing for sand-eels in the water close to the shore. These are elegant swallow-shaped sea-birds like gulls and very skilled fliers. They patrol about 6–8m above the sea, spying for small fish near the surface. When they spot one, they quickly dive with closed wings to catch it with their sharp beaks. You can sometimes see the silver glint of the fish when the tern emerges from the water. Males aim to impress their mates by offering them fish to show off their hunting skills.

Sand means sandcastles, but really there are all sorts of variations you could try. What about a hobbit village? Damp sand is the best for building – it holds its shape better. And you can use anything you find along the beach to help frame buildings or to decorate them. Seaweed, stones, shells, old plastic containers, old fishing nets can all be used as building materials or decoration. But it is probably best to avoid metal things, since they can have sharp edges.

Keep a look out for nice pebbles and shells and maybe even sea-washed glass. You can use them for making patterns in the sand or making necklaces and bracelets and decorating things back home. Sea-washed glass usually has any sharp edges rounded off through erosion by sand (just like sandpaper on wood), but it is best to check.

▲ Terns patrol
shallow water by
beaches and dive
down to catch
small fish.

Nature Safari

project

making jewellery

You can make your own necklaces or bracelets from all sorts of objects from the natural world.

You will need:
Any interesting objects you can find – shells, small pieces of driftwood, seeds, leaves
Cotton thread
Needle
Leather, cord, string, raffia to thread your objects on to

Try to find shells that already have holes in them – drilling holes in shells can be difficult. It is a good idea to give leaves a coat of varnish first, as this gives them shine and strength.

Thread the seeds and leaves onto a length of cotton and then tie this at intervals to the cord or thong you are using for your necklace or bracelet. Larger objects such as shells or small pieces of wood can be threaded directly onto the cord. You can add beads in with the natural objects if you want to.

Dunes

▲ Sand dunes are constantly changing shape with the wind.

Wind shapes the sand dunes, like gigantic ripples or waves on the surface of water. And the dunes actually move very gradually, year by year, down wind. The wind blows small amounts of sand off the top of a dune ridge to settle on the more sheltered side, so the pile of the dune slowly moves forward. The highest sand dunes in the world rise to about 400m high and are in the Sahara desert.

Various hardy grasses and reeds can survive in the shifting sands of more stable areas and their roots help to bind patches of sand together, so other plants can begin to grow. Then further back from the sea there is usually a fuller community of plants interspersed with more open patches and sometimes ponds in lower hollows. This can be a very good area for various wildlife.

▼ Yellow rattle – a common flower of sand dunes.

There are some beautiful wild flowers that are common on dunes from spring to summer. Cowslips, bloody cranesbill, viper's bugloss are some of the more poetic names. These flowering dunes should have a good scent to them at this time of year too. Butterflies, beetles, grasshoppers and other insects should be easy to find in favoured hollows. Small blue and copper butterflies are often found in the dunes. If you are lucky AND you can prowl as stealthily as a cat, you may find some lizards basking in the sun.

Nature Safari

Rockpooling

How long have people enjoyed hunting in rockpools? Probably as long as humans have headed for the seaside in the heat of the summer. A rockpool is a fascinating self-contained world on a scale that's easy to grasp. Very few are completely devoid of life and many contain a whole range of creatures, some strange-looking, some a little scary, some that may give you a little nip, but very few are dangerous – at least in north and west Europe.

▲ A clear rockpool – approach slowly so as not to scare any small fish.

A rockpool is a miniature, marooned sea left by the falling tide; twice a day it becomes part of the sea again as the tide returns and changes the water.

Most of the animals will dive for cover as soon as the figure of a human looms over the pool. Sometimes it pays to creep up on a pool; or if you can be patient, sit very still beside the pool (without casting a shadow) and the animals will gradually emerge again.

Other creatures prefer to skulk under rocks, under clumps of seaweed or hidden in ledges. A short stick is useful for brushing obstacles aside or gently prodding in crevices. Try lifting some rocks over – watch out for crabs or small fish racing away and starfish clinging to the underside of the rock. But remember to replace the rock carefully as it was – without crushing anything.

Links

catching tiddlers p.78

Things to look for

Crabs, hermit crabs, shrimps, starfish, sea-slaters, sea-anemones, small fish like blennies and small eels, limpets, barnacles, periwinkles, mussels, beautiful rosy-pink coralweed – stranded jellyfish!
Occasionally larger fish and octopuses get stranded in rockpools; so be prepared for a surprise.

project

diary

See how many different kinds of animal you can find. A net and a bucket are the only tools you will need: it is great fun to try to catch some of the creatures and then you can take a closer look at them. See if you can look a crab in the eye – if you can recognise its eyes! Later you can put the names of what you caught in your diary and maybe do a drawing of your favourite discovery.

But look after the creatures you catch: they all have their own place in the world and some of them may be rare. Many of them cannot live without water; but don't leave them in a bucket or a small pool or with no cover for too long – it may become stifling for them, especially if the water warms up.

Check the local paper. In the summer, the National Trust, local wildlife trusts and local countryside services often hold rockpooling sessions with an experienced guide. A little local knowledge is always very useful and then you can go off and do your own thing with confidence.

Mermaids

Stories have been told for many years in countries all over the world about creatures, rather like humans, living in the sea. In our part of the world there are tales of mermaids who have bodies with the top half of a woman and the bottom half like the tail of a fish. Mermaids are shy creatures, frightened of people so are rarely seen; but many old fishermen have seen or heard them. So, if you are on the rocks and you hear some soft wailing voices, or see some big dark eyes looking at you from the sea, it's probably a seal – but take a good look just in case!

When and where

Parts of the coast where small sandy or shingle beaches are interspersed with gently shelving jumbles of rock, are probably the best places to explore rock pools. Summer is the best season, since there is more life to see in the pools and it's not so cold if you get wet. Around high tide there are no pools to explore. The pools furthest from the sea are often smelly with decomposing seaweed, as they are not cleaned out by the tide very often. The pools at mid-height and towards the low tide mark are usually the best; but keep an eye on the tide, so that you don't get surrounded as it comes in. The less wind there is, the better, since the wind ruffles the water surface making it harder to see in.

Links

for making a viewer to see underwater more clearly, see pond viewer p.125

Take care

- Remember you'll probably get wet, so take a change of clothes with you.
- Seaside rocks are often very slippery – even when they are not covered in seaweed. DO NOT RUN OR JUMP.
- Be alert for the tide coming in and be careful not to get stranded.
- It is best not to put your hands too far under rocks as you never know what might be there!
- Pick up a small crab from behind with your thumb and first finger across the broadest part of its back – then it can't get its claws at you.

◄ The pincers of a large crab can give a powerful nip.

Harbours

▲ Harbour waters are always worth a look for fish and crabs.

▼ Seabirds are attracted to fishing boats for the scraps thrown overboard.

The harbours of small towns and villages work like a magnet on me. I love to see fishing boats arriving. Most fishing fleets now work from larger centres where it can be difficult and even dangerous to watch them easily, but there are still plenty of smaller villages and ports with working boats and these can be good to visit.

Often boats arriving back have a whole flock of gulls following, on the look-out for any scraps thrown overboard. Their wails and shrieks echo from the surrounding buildings. The bold ones come down onto the deck to pick out any small fish still stuck in the folded nets with their strong beaks. Watch out for the large gulls lining the pier or roofs – the herring gulls and the great black-backed gulls; every so often one will put on a display, throwing back its head and calling out with its loud, laughing song.

Nature Safari

You can usually get to see what's been caught while the fishermen are unloading the crates of fish from the boat. If there's a market by the harbour, that's another good place to see what unusual creatures have been brought in. See if there's an angler-fish there: fish-sellers often call them monkfish now, but 'angler' fish is a better description of how it lives. It lies motionless on the sea bed and the short stick-like thing on its head attracts little fish looking for food; but as they approach, the angler-fish makes a sudden lunge, opens wide its enormous mouth and the little fish becomes its food.

Links

fish p.75

If there is a car park where people eat their fish and chips, there will probably be a flock of black-headed gulls hanging out around the edges, waiting for any scraps. The bolder ones might take a chip from your hand – they will surely land on your car. Check out their blood-red beaks and the white eye-rings on their dark chocolate hoods.

Starlings are usually common around harbours. When they are singing in the sun, their feathers glint with a hundred colours. They are pretty good singers too. The famous composer Mozart used to keep a pet starling from which he copied some of his tunes. He was so fond of the bird that he held an elaborate funeral when it died.

Starlings are great mimics and in their songs you can hear copies of the calls of other birds. They have also taken to copying phone ring-tones and car alarms, so listen out – the copies are usually a bit quieter than the real thing.

Look out for cormorants on rocks and piers, holding their wings out to dry and looking like black pterodactyls.

Among the fish catch

Large crabs, prawns, lobsters, plaice, sole, herring, mackerel, cod, halibut, ling, squid

▶ Starlings often perch on aerials and chimneys.

Rivers and ponds

The water on our planet is constantly on the move. Rain falls on the land and the force of gravity draws it ever down to sea level; you can easily see the water flowing in rivers, but ponds and lakes slow its journey. Some water seeps into the ground and may be taken up by plants or join very slowly moving underground reservoirs. Warmth from the sun raises moisture from the seas to form rain clouds and the cycle goes on.

On its journey, water provides a living environment for many creatures, is drunk by all plants and animals, is channelled into our cities for various uses and is dammed to provide electricity and to water crops. We also use rivers and seas for our waste and when we put too much waste in, either deliberately or accidentally, it becomes polluted to the point where it is unfit for life. Some of the main pollutants that effect water quality are sewage, fertilisers, oil and waste gases, which are picked up by rain clouds in the atmosphere.

▶ Rivers provide a habitat for many different creatures

Rivers and ponds are great places for observing wildlife. Not only is there the world of the *aquatic* creatures beneath the surface, the divided world of *amphibians* and many insects who live the first half of their lives in water, but the watersides provide a home and food for many kinds of land animals. Since all land animals need water to drink, they regularly visit places where they can drink in safety.

Even in areas where the surrounding land is intensively farmed, the banks of rivers and ponds are usually left to grow wild and have a more natural character. The plants here include those kinds that need wet ground like reeds and sedges, but trees also line the water's edge where the ground is firm enough. Some plants even grow in the water itself, such as water lilies in still water or crowfoot in swifter streams. Often paths follow the banks of rivers, ponds and lakes, so these are good places to go for wildlife walks – provided you watch where you put your feet.

▲ Water lilies – floating leaves and stunning flowers.

Links

catching tiddlers p.78 and for making your own pond, see wildlife gardening p.95

project

pond dipping

You will need:
Fishing net
Jar
Small dish
Magnifying glass
A suction tube or dropper is useful too, for collecting the more microscopic creatures

One of the best ways of getting to see what is living in and on any pond, is by pond dipping: you draw a net through the water, then take a look at what is in it. Scientists would call this 'taking a random sample'. It is best to have a water container with you, ideally a large jar, for putting any larger items in that you catch. Then you can get a good look at them. Fill the jar with water from the pond if you can: this is the water that the animals are used to and you may see small shrimps and insects in it. Smaller items and scoops of pond water can also be put in the dish for a closer look.

Remember that many creatures that live in water cannot survive for very long out of it; fish should be put back into water within half a minute at the longest. Try not to catch too much water weed in your net – it is not good for the net or the pond.

There are some ponds which don't have much living in them; because of pollution or for some other reason the water is not suitable. But most ponds are teeming with life from spring to summer; much of it is on a miniature, or even microscopic scale, but there should be plenty visible with a naked, beady eye.

What's in a pond?

There are many different kinds of underwater and surface insects that you might come across, some of them quite large: the water boatman is quite common and there are various large diving beetles. Occasionally, you may come across the giants of this world: the great diving beetle, the water scorpion, the water stick insect – these are some of the largest insects of northern Europe. The long tail of the water scorpion is not a sting, but a breathing tube. In fact it isn't really a scorpion at all and has got its name just because it looks a bit like a scorpion.

Stranger-looking insects include the larvae of various flies, particularly mosquitoes. The monsters of this group are the larvae of the great diving beetle and dragonfly larvae – all greedy predators that feed on tadpoles and will even go for small fish if they get the chance.

Some ponds support large populations of water snails; you may find all sizes from the very young to large adults. Snails play an important role in the pond community by grazing on the algae (slimy green weed) that begins to grow over all surfaces in summer.

▲ The larva of the great diving beetle – a fierce pond predator.

Fish, newts and frogs are harder to catch; if you do try to catch these faster-moving creatures, be careful not to hurt them by crushing them with the net frame; and do not keep them out of water in sunshine for too long, as this will harm them.

There are some quite creepy creatures among the pond dwellers: leeches and hair-worms are two kinds of parasite that feed off other insects and fish. Hair-worms look just like a long piece of thin hair, but you'll see it curling and slowly wriggling if it's alive.

Early spring is a good time to visit a pond. Anytime from the end of January on, depending on how far north you are, frogs and toads will be gathering on their breeding ponds and this the time for frog spawn. On milder days and evenings you should hear a good croaking chorus of male frogs and the bleeping of toads.

Always remember to wash your hands after you've been mucking about with pond water.

Links

frog spawn p.57

Bugs on ponds

Surface tension – when you are small and lightweight this is the force you can use to patrol the surface of a sheet of water. And it is more slippery than a sheet of ice. Pond skaters have mastered the art of speed ON water. Watch them go!

They hold still for a time like miniature oil platforms on stilts, but when they move it is sudden and fast. Stretch your hand over them and see them scatter to a safe distance. They live by feeding on the insect casualties from the aerial world – the flies and suchlike that fall in the water and can't swim.

If pond skaters take the prize for speed, whirlygig beetles, in the shiny suits, get the dancing prize. As their name suggests, they whirl around each other, massed together

▲ Pond skater.

▶ Water boatman.

Links

dragonflies p.61

Nature Safari

project

make a pond viewer

You can easily make a pond viewer to see things below the surface of the water more clearly.

You will need:
Large clear plastic bottle
Clear plastic bag
Strong elastic band
Scissors

1. Ask an adult to cut the top and bottom off the plastic bottle.
2. Stretch the plastic bag over one end of the bottle. Fix it in place with the elastic band.
3. Carefully lower your viewer into the water and look through the plastic bottom. Can you see any snails or tadpoles?

on a pool's surface. This makes it hard to keep your eyes on any single one and thereby confuses predators.

Another insect with special skills is the water boatman. This one is a champion diver. It rests hanging under the surface taking in air, then suddenly sweeps away with two elongated legs like oars, diving into the depths of its pool to look for food.

It is easy to forget something about these insects that are so at home in water – they also fly. The most spectacular of all flying insects spends its early life as a beetle-like larva in the water, then in its adult life is often found around water: the dragonfly. When the larva is ready to change into an adult, it crawls up onto some waterside vegetation, where the adult dragonfly emerges from its shell and dries in the air.

Fish

Bridges make good observation points; often you can see into the water below and spot fish. You can drop a small stick into the stream below and watch it go under the bridge and then down-stream to get an idea of how fast the current is, which can sometimes be deceptive.

You can try feeding the fish. Bread will attract minnows in streams, if they are there; in park ponds there are often very large carp that will come and take bread from the surface. There are places where people regularly feed fish and there can often be quite a large shoal hanging around the area waiting for an easy meal. Small pieces of bread will float; you can try rolling a larger piece into a ball so that it will sink and maybe attract some different fish. Or, on a quiet stream, you can just watch: if a wasp, a moth or another insect falls on the surface and its struggling sends out ripples, there is a good chance that some fish will be attracted to snap it up.

▼ Minnow – a common small fish of flowing water.

► Carp – a large fish of still water.

Think from the fish's point of view, looking up from beneath the surface and watching out for all those predatory creatures in the airy world above, hungry for a fishy dinner. Don't let your shadow fall on water and try not to present your outline against the sky; try creeping up slowly to a likely looking spot. Tread lightly on the bank or gently in the water, since fish and many other creatures are sensitive to the slightest vibrations in the water and the ground. Sunglasses can help reduce surface glare where light from the sun or a bright sky is reflected on the surface of water.

Nature Safari

Birds

Look out for herons fishing in the shallow water in the edges. They stand in the water on their long legs keeping very still, until some small fish is a little unwary and comes too close; then they strike with their dagger-like beak at lightning speed. If you are lucky you may see a heron catch a larger fish, and struggle to swallow it; it takes some time for the bulge to go down the heron's narrow neck.

Look out also for kingfishers. They sit on a branch just above the surface, then dive in when a small fish swims by. Often all you see of kingfishers is the flash of emerald-blue and flame-red as they dash over the water. Further north, in the faster streams, lives a bird that 'flies' underwater looking for insects under stones – the dipper.

▲ The kingfisher dives for fish.

On larger ponds and slow rivers, coots are common. They are all black except for their white beak, which extends up onto their foreheads – hence the phrase 'bald as a coot'. They feed mainly on water plants and can be very noisy when neighbours get too close; they make loud 'keck' calls and chase off across the surface of the water in a splashing run. See if you can get a look at their feet: not fully webbed like a duck, but with webbing around all their toes – very good for walking on soggy surfaces.

◄ The heron thrusts forward its long beak to catch fish.

Waterfalls & eddies

Links

salmon p.76

Rivers and streams in hilly areas are usually faster flowing than in flat areas; they also have more waterfalls on them. Small waterfalls may have good swimming pools beneath them, but make sure you have an adult with you and get their permission before going in the water. In the autumn you can sometimes see migratory fish like salmon jumping at smaller waterfalls, trying to get further upstream to spawn.

Scattered about in the higher hills are some spectacular waterfalls, some hundreds of feet high. If you are in hill country try to find out if there is a good one nearby. Be careful near high waterfalls: they are usually bordered by some very steep ground and nearby stones can be slippery or loose.

Watch the eddies in swifter rivers and streams. These are the small whirlpools formed at the edge of the main current, where the flow gets turned back on itself. You can throw a small stick in and watch its progress, to see how the current flows in a stream.

▼ A fine stream for dam-building.

Tracks & signs

Keep an eye out for holes in the bank, which may be a kingfisher's nest, or if there are many, a sand martin colony. They may be a sign of bank voles, harmless plant-eaters of the waterside and good swimmers. Some people mistake them for rats ('water rats'), but their face is rounded with a blunt nose, not pointed. They used to be very common until quite recently, but North American mink, originally escaped from fur farms, have wiped them out in many areas.

Patches of sand or mud on the edge are good places to look for footprints. Mammal footprints need a bit of practise to tell apart, but you could try to work out what kind of animal might have made the print. Animals like otters, stoats, foxes, mink and badgers can all be recognised from their droppings as well. It's all right – you don't have to touch them! Just may be smell them. There are good books to help with recognising tracks and other signs.

Links

animal tracks and signs p.146

▼ What kind of animal might have left this track?

project

make a water wheel

You will need:
Foil dish
Stick or string
Scissors

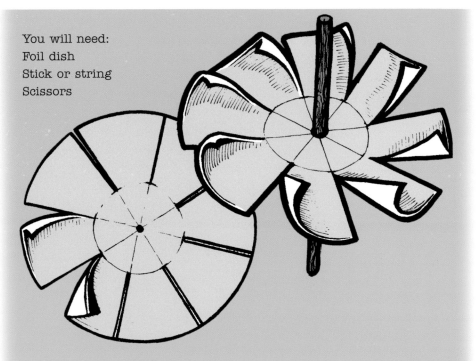

1. Cut a small circle from the base of the foil dish.
2. Make eight cuts into the centre, stopping a few centimetres from the centre.
3. Curve up the edge of each section, making sure the curved pieces are pointing in the same direction.
4. Thread the string or stick through the centre of the wheel.
5. Hold in a running stream or under the tap to see the water turn the wheel.

Safety

So rivers and ponds are great places for exploring and generally messing about; but there are potential dangers to be wary of and top of the list is FALLING IN.

Just like at the swimming pool, you really shouldn't run around the edges of ponds or along the banks of rivers. Banks may be weak and give way; there may be burrows of voles or rabbits, hidden by grasses, to trip you up; there may also be strong currents in a river.

Be alert for river levels rising, especially in hilly areas. There may have been a heavy rainstorm a little further upstream, or water may have been released from a dam. Either way, if you notice the river level rising, back off to somewhere away from the water's edge and well above the level of the river. In some circumstances, gentle streams can become raging torrents in a matter of minutes.

If you enjoy spending time around water – learn to swim.

Also, be careful of muddy areas (getting stuck), jumping onto stones (that are wet, slimy and slippery), stepping onto stones in water (wobbly) and trying to stretch just that little bit too far with a fishing net (and losing your balance!).

As a general rule, it is better not to drink any water – certainly not pond water. The lower parts of rivers are often quite dirty; higher up, nearer the source, a stream should be cleaner, but you never know – there may be a dead sheep or a dead deer lying in the water further up-stream.

◀ Be careful that you don't slip when spending time near water

Meadows, heaths and moors

▲ The word 'moor' comes from an old Gaelic word meaning the big place.

What connects these three habitats is that they are all open places, mostly clear of trees. There may be a few trees growing here and there, or even a wood, but most of the area will be covered by quite low vegetation. In the case of moors and heaths, the characteristic plants are various types of heather and ecologists define these habitats as 'dwarf shrub heaths'. These heaths tend to develop where the underlying soil lacks nutrition for other plants. Meadows develop on richer soils, especially in river valleys, and are made up of long grasses and a range of flowering herbs.

Nature Safari

Now here's something to think about: almost all moors, heaths and meadows were once covered by trees and would return to being forest if it wasn't for one thing – humans. They are the result of years of clearance by our fires in the past and grazing by farm animals, especially sheep (and some wild animals).

Although these are open habitats from our point of view, the dense but low cover of the grasses and shrubs, offers a sheltered world to a whole range of smaller animals including snakes and lizards, small mammals like voles, various birds, like grouse and partridges, and especially insects and spiders.

Skylarks and meadow pipits are typical birds of all these habitats, though they prefer the grassier areas of heaths and moors, and where meadows are not too overgrown or wet. The males of both species take to the air to advertise their presence. Whereas the skylark pours out a stream of chirruping from high up, the meadow pipit rises to about tree height piping away, then glides back to earth with a cascade of twittering.

▲ Skylarks are at home running along the ground; but they sing from high in the air.

Meadows, heaths and moors

Moors and heaths

Heather, bracken, gorse bushes, birch trees, peaty soils, bogs, mosses, snakes and lizards, spiders, grasshoppers, dragonflies, grouse, wheatears, whinchats and stonechats, nightjars, carnivorous plants, birds of prey.

▲ Heather flowering in August turns moors and heaths purple.

People have always thought of moors and heaths as mysterious landscapes: they have usually been portrayed as wastelands, where one can easily get lost, a lonely place to live and where strange things happen. In poor weather conditions, they are desolate, providing little shelter for a traveller. But to sit by a moorland stream on a spring afternoon or a warm summer evening, can make such places feel very welcoming and full of life.

The lack of trees and generally short vegetation gives these habitats an openness that you can sense. They are often on undulating or even hilly land and this leads the eye into the depth of distance: you can enjoy watching a buzzard circling in the sky even when it is 1km away. Moors and heaths are places of individual charm and beauty.

Moors and heaths develop on poor soils, which *ecologists* call acidic. They are lacking in the *nutrients* necessary for many plants and many soil *invertebrates,* like worms. Because there are very few invertebrates to eat through old vegetation, it decomposes very slowly into peat, the dark soil characteristic of these areas. There can be large areas of boggy ground as well as small pockets. They are usually full of a kind of moss called sphagnum, which can often look like a firm surface, so take care.

Nature Safari

Watch out for adders on moors and heaths. They are common in some places, though they can be difficult to see since they avoid people when possible and are sensitive to the vibrations of our approaching footsteps. In March and April, when they first emerge from their winter hibernation, they like to bask in sheltered spots on sunny days. At this time they are slower to move off and in certain areas it is worth being alert for their zig-zag pattern (see p.53).

Lizards can be common in heather; but like the adders that hunt them, they are quick and you need to be alert or lucky to spot one before it sees you and darts off. Also like adders, they are slower in the spring and cool weather, since they rely on the sun for warmth and a warmer body allows quicker reactions and motion.

You may see some large rusty-coloured moths zipping over the heather during spring and summer: there is a good chance that these will be emperor moths – beautiful creatures, but very difficult to observe at rest; usually they stop for just a moment and then fly on. You can recognise the males by their feathery antennae, very sensitive to the scent of a female: if you can approach one close enough to tell whether it is male or female, you really are becoming a good tracker.

▲ Emperor moth female.

The golden-ringed dragonfly, a large and spectacular species, can be common on moorland and heathland streams in summer. It often patrols at quite a low level along the stream; if you see one dipping repeatedly onto the edge of the stream, it is probably a female laying eggs. Try to take a closer look.

Meadows, heaths and moors

Tiger beetles

During the summer keep an eye out for the tiger beetle on patches of bare ground on heaths and moors. It is a fast runner (one of the fastest insects), so you will need to be sharp, and it can take flight. This is a fierce predator in its miniature world, catching other smaller insects with its speed. Deadly in its own world, but harmless to us, it is rather beautiful with the shiny green design on its wing-cases (ie. its back).

Want to catch a tiger beetle? Try using a fishing net. And if you've got a specimen jar, put it in there. You could then illustrate the pattern on the beetle's back in your notebook or diary; or you could do a large-scale drawing of the whole beetle, including its jaws.

▼ Green tiger Beetle – an insect sprinter.

Spider's webs

Moors and heaths are good places to take a look at spiders' webs – often spread across a gap in the heather or strung from the branches of a low bush. They are easier to see in the early morning, when the sun is low and they may be lined with dew. There are several different designs used.

You could try gently vibrating the web with a piece of grass. Be careful not to break the threads. This should bring the spider out from its hiding place at the edge of the web to investigate. If you are lucky, you may see a fly get caught in the web and watch the spider come out to deal with it – either eat it or wrap it in more threads to secure it for later.

Nature Safari

Deer

The early morning and evening in summer are good times to see deer in these habitats. Roe deer come out of the woods into the open to feed; and red deer come down from the higher ground to drink and feed by moorland streams.

▼ Roe deer in the early morning sunshine.

Birds of prey

Moors and heaths can be good places to see birds of prey. Various falcons hunt these habitats and buzzards are generally quite common. If you are lucky, you may see a golden eagle soaring high over the moors in a mountain region. Where there are bogs and ponds on heathland, watch out for dashing small falcons called hobbies, hunting dragonflies. They swoop down into a fast glide, grab the dragonfly in their talons with a sudden twist in flight and eat it while still on the wing.

◀ Hobby – dashing and acrobatic in flight.

Links

stalking p.144

Meadows, heaths and moors

137

Meadows

▲ A good meadow for wildlife.

Meadowlands have plant communities made up of various grasses and flowering herbs. Some meadows are quite marshy and these often have plants similar to a riverside including rushes and sedges; grasses and herbs dominate meadows on drier soils. In many areas the meadows have changed or disappeared completely over the last century. Many have been taken for farming and turned to fields for stocking animals or growing crops. Older meadows were maintained by light grazing and are much richer in plant species. They support an abundance of insects, from spiders and harvestmen through to hoverflies and butterflies.

▼ A Grass Snake living in the walls of a barn.

Waterside meadows are good places to find grass snakes, though they are not easily seen unless they are sunning themselves in an open spot or swimming. Grass snakes frequently hunt the water's edge and in the water itself. In some places, locals call them 'water snakes'.

Brown and blue butterflies of a variety of species are common on flower-rich meadows. It can be very difficult to identify them; one thing they have in common is that nearly all of them have marks on their wings that look like the eyes of a small bird, a weasel or even a snake.

A meadowland moth that is easily mistaken for a butterfly in flight is the red underwing. They can be hard to spot when they are in the grass with their wings folded: they look just like a dead leaf or a piece of twig. But if they are disturbed, they take to the air and fly off, showing their back wings which are red with a black band. So they have a good name.

Meadows, and the grassier areas in heather, can be excellent spots for grasshoppers. Grasshoppers like sunshine and warmth, so July through to September are the best times to see them – and hear them. In southern areas you may also come across their close relatives, bush-crickets and crickets; they both have long antennae and have chirping or whirring songs.

In the late evening some of the night birds can be seen as they come out to hunt over the meadows. Barn owls slowly and silently patrol just above the grasses listening for voles to pounce on. If you are lucky you may hear one give its ghostly shriek. In the past they've been called 'screech-owls' and some people thought the calls were from the spirits of the dead.

▲ Barn owl.

Links

mimicry p.40

Where there are trees nearby, especially on heathlands, you may catch sight of a small hawk-like bird flitting about in the twilight. Nightjars are big-eyed moth hunters, with big bristling mouths to help catch these and other large night-flying insects. More likely you'll hear the male's strange song, like a distant motorbike, hypnotically rising and falling in pitch. This is another night bird that superstitious people were afraid of in the past; its old name 'goat-sucker' will give you an idea of what they thought it got up to during the night.

▶ Nightjar – perfectly camouflaged when resting on the ground in day-time.

Links

map reading p.161

Safety

Be careful of bracken. It can be fun to try to get through when it is green and high – a jungle world of its own – and can make good den walls when it is dead and dry. But it is tough and stringy once fully grown, and when it is dead it's easy to get a nasty cut from it. Never pull it too hard in case your hand slips along it.

It's easy to keep wandering on in these open spaces, which are often criss-crossed by paths. Unless you've followed a feature like a stream or the edge of a wood, it can be very easy to get lost, and on the higher moorlands the weather can change quite suddenly. Keep an eye on your surroundings and remember any turns you make. If you want to go for a longer walk ask an adult to come along and use a map; if you can't read a map, take a companion who can, until you learn. If you plan to go on longer walks, you should also learn to use a compass, so you won't be caught out by misty weather.

A menace

You should be aware that animals like sheep and deer (large grazing animals) have their parasites (see p.31). There's one in particular that's quite common throughout these habitats, a tiny nasty little insect with such an innocent sounding name – a tick.

They are blood-suckers and though their main victims may be deer or sheep, they seem quite happy to get their heads stuck into dogs and human flesh!

◄ Ticks are nasty creatures that can cause Lyme's disesase in humans.

They bide their time on a twig in the vegetation until some animal brushes past, when they grab a hold on the fur (or socks, jumper, hair...). They crawl slowly into the fur until they find some warm bare flesh and then they quite literally get their heads stuck in. They slowly drink a little blood from their host and over a period of days their bodies swell to maybe 10 times the size.

You have to be careful when removing a tick not to leave the head behind stuck in the flesh, where it can become infected. They come off fairly easily in the first day or so, when they are just getting settled and their bodies are small, but it gets trickier later.

The ticks themselves may be unpleasant, but they are not particularly dangerous. Ticks in some areas are in their turn the hosts for an even more minute parasite – a virus, which they can pass on to humans who then develop Lyme's disease. This is very serious – but fortunately not common.

Tracking
skills

Approaching wild creatures

The first thing to be aware of is that, from a wild animal's point of view, you are a threat – a danger. The way of life in the wild is very much a matter of life and death on a daily basis. Most kinds of animal are potential food for some predator; the large predators, at the top of the food chain, usually come into conflict with humans' farming and hunting interests and are thus wary of people.

This is true at least for almost all the animals of Europe. Individuals of just a few species may stand their ground when facing a human; many more may bite, kick or defend themselves in some other way if cornered or handled. In general, animals around their breeding site or with young close by, tend to be bolder and more prone to attack – typical parental instincts, ask yours!

Fulmars, small members of the albatross family that nest on Europe's coastal outcrops, project a shot of semi-digested liquid fish at anyone who approaches their nest too close – a sticky, foul-smelling surprise for any intruder.

So, a certain amount of stealth is usually required to approach creatures in the wild, but bear in mind that there are circumstances when you shouldn't approach too close. Wasps may be interesting creatures, but it is not a good idea to peer too closely into the entrance of a wasps' nest. At least not while it's in use (mainly June to October).

Ten guide-lines for finding and watching wildlife

1. Move slowly and quietly.
2. Wear colours that match your surroundings.
3. Try going out early in the morning or late in the evening.
4. Be patient and don't be too disappointed if you don't find something first time.
5. Use your ears as well as your eyes.
6. Research your subject's habits.
7. Sit for while in what seems a good place.
8. Talk quietly.
9. Don't be afraid to ask for advice.
10. Think about what you see and why it is the way it is.

Stalking

▲ Use tree trunks and bushes for cover.

When you are out somewhere that seems good for wildlife, move more slowly and quietly, while looking and listening for signs. When you see something, stop still. Check it is not watching you (and about to leap off). When it starts feeding again, or cleaning itself, take a few more steps. Animals tend to see movement better than still shapes, so the best technique is to move in slow motion (no sudden jerks), when the animal is not looking at you directly.

Use hollows in the land, tree trunks and bushes to screen yourself while walking closer. Bend lower so your silhouette does not break the skyline. If you get serious, you may need to get down and crawl – uncomfortable and messy, but it works.

I once approached a wild otter like this on the shores of a lake – I was so close, I began to think it might be a tame one. So I whistled softly, making a motion towards it, and suddenly shattered the illusion: the animal shot off into the water and dived, only resurfacing a good way out.

Most mammals have a good sense of smell, so it is best to approach from downwind of them (i.e. with the wind blowing from them to you). Otherwise they will 'get wind of you' and probably move off in the other direction.

project

camouflage hide-and-seek

Why not try a game of hide-and-seek in a wood or among scattered bushes? To make it more testing, everyone should aim to camouflage themselves so that they are almost invisible among grasses, branches and leaves.

Colour scheme helps – duller shades with no bold outlines work best in general. But the aim is to blend in with the natural background or surroundings. If you can, keep to the shadows – out of bright sunlight and try to avoid approaching something or some water with the sun full in your face. A peaked cap can be useful for casting a shadow over your face as well as keeping the sun out of your eyes on a bright day.

When looking into a pond or a river, think fish-eye. What does it see above the water's surface. The easiest thing for it to detect is a moving silhouette against the skyline and the fish will dart for cover to escape the alien menace. So try to avoid appearing like a weird monster!

Animal tracks and signs

Skin and bones

▲ Feathers and cones are good wildlife clues.

▶ The skull of a roe deer buck, found in a wood.

TIP • TIP

• Use a stick if you want to move any animal remains or look under them.

If you are not put off by dead things (with sometimes a little blood or maybe a nasty smell), they are of great interest to a naturalist – nature's detective, looking for clues and examining the victim, just like any inspector. Though it is sad that they are dead, it's also an opportunity to see shy animals close-up.

Sometimes you might find the bones or even a full skeleton of an animal. The skull is the best piece for identifying an animal, though it is rarely easy. A look at the teeth could tell you whether the animal was a hunter and a meat eater (sharp and spiky) or a plant eater (flatter, with several points for chewing and maybe two long front teeth for gnawing). Many animals have a mixture of both to cope with a varied diet.

Fish skeletons are easily identified: a long backbone with several rows of much finer bones running along it. Often the head will still be attached since this is very bony.

Nature Safari

Feathers

Birds grow a new set of feathers at least once each year and during this time their old ones fall out – not all at once, that would be a disaster, but gradually over different areas of their bodies, so there is only ever a few feathers missing at one time. When birds renew their feathers or mammals change their fur, it is called moulting.

Most of the feathers we see lying around are from moulting or just odd feathers that a bird has lost. If you find a clump of feathers, there is probably more to it: either a bird has bumped into something or it has had a brush with a predator. If there are quite a lot of feathers together, then it is likely that a predator has caught the bird, spat some out and maybe started to pluck its prey.

Cats, foxes, hawks and falcons all catch birds as prey. By thinking about the location of the remains and examining the quill ends of the feathers, you can make a guess at the hunter's identity. Chewed quills suggest a fox; neatly clipped ones suggest a sparrowhawk.

If you are familiar with birds, you might be able to make a good guess at what species of bird the feathers are from. Some can be very distinctive, such as the blue feathers from a jay's wing-patch, many of the feathers of a male pheasant or the banded grey, white and sometimes black from a woodpigeon.

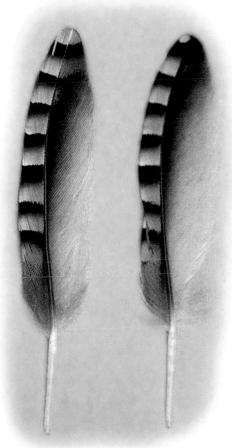

▲ Feathers from the wing patch of a jay.

Some feathers have lovely patterns on them. You could build your own collection of feathers either to help with identification or just for their varied beauty. Small ones can be taped into a notebook or diary.

Footprints

► Badger paw prints embedded in the earth

It is not easy to identify the species or animal from just their footprints, but you can usually get an idea of what size of animal or bird made them. Look in damp sand or mud alongside water; this keeps a print well and is visited by waterside creatures, including otters in suitable areas, and other animals coming to drink.

▼ Rabbit tracks in the snow

One of the best times for investigating animal tracks is when there's been a fresh fall of snow overnight. Get out early before it becomes riddled with other people's footprints and see what is there. This can be really interesting, even in a small urban garden; if a fox has been through, it will have left its trail of prints, like a dog's but narrower, usually evenly spaced from its steady trot. You will have to learn to tell it apart from the footprints of prowling cats.

Nature Safari

project

printing tracks

To print your own animal tracks on paper, you will need:

Plain paper for printing on to
A medium to large potato
A knife
A shallow dish or paper plate
Paints
Paint brush
Felt-tip pen

1. Choose the animal track you want to print – see below for some ideas to try.
2. Cut the potato in half and dry it.
3. Draw the outline of the footprint onto the potato with felt pen.
4. Get an adult to help you carve away the potato from around the foot print.
5. Either dip the potato into a shallow dish of paint, or paint onto it with a brush.
6. Make your prints on the paper.

It is not just the paw print itself that gives you a clue to the animal that made it, but the pattern of the footfalls. Rabbits leave a very characteristic pattern of their four feet from the way they hop about. The fox's footprints mentioned above would be in a very different pattern, bunched together in fours, if the animal was running.

Bird footprints usually have three forward-facing toes and one to the rear, all spreading from a point. But ducks and geese have only a short rear claw that sometimes leaves no print at all, and there should be a slight print of the webbing between their front claws.

Droppings and pellets

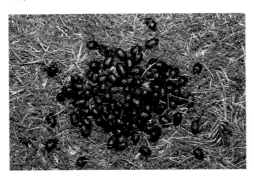

You can also learn to recognise the droppings of different mammals. The vegetarians tend to produce roundish, firm and fibrous droppings, very small from a vole, marble-sized from a deer. Carnivores produce longer, tube-shaped droppings, often thinning at an end. Otters' and minks' droppings have a pungent fishy smell, whereas pine martens' are said to be sweet and musty.

After eating, certain predators spit out the indigestible parts of the prey as pellets, mainly composed of hair and bone (see p.34). These can be found where birds of prey perch to digest their meals.

Pine cones

Several animals are able to prise the seeds out of pine cones for food, but usually it is the work of squirrels or crossbills. Squirrels chew the cone down to a core, crossbills prise open the scales.

◄► Pine cone, before and after a squirrel has been chewing one.

Birds' nests

Birds' nests can last a long time after they've been used; some even get used again the following year by a different species. Some nests are quite distinctive. Magpie's nests have a domed roof of twigs; rooks nest in a colony (usually very noisy), whereas carrion crows are solitary nesters; song thrushes' nests have a lining of mud and wrens' are a ball of moss or dead leaves with a hole at the side.

If you find a nest that is being used, don't hang around nearby for too long. You may keep the parents from the nest and the eggs will chill or the young ones go hungry; sometimes parents will desert a nest if disturbed too much.

Holes in the ground

Very small holes are usually the work of mice and voles. Sometimes there may be a hole to a mole's tunnel, but the heaped soil of molehills are a more obvious sign of their presence. Small holes in a river bank could be the nests of sand martins or a kingfisher, or just possibly the rare bank vole. Medium-sized holes are usually rabbit burrows; rabbit holes are often found in groups with little piles of soil or sand outside. If they are rabbit holes, there will be small oval-shaped droppings, about 1cm long, lying around.

Larger holes may be fox dens or badger setts; foxes sometimes take over badger setts. Badgers tend to live in larger extended family groups than foxes, though they all tend to hunt for food on their own. Badger setts usually have a quite a few entrances several metres apart, leading through tunnels to sleeping chambers. At least some of the entrances have mounds of earth outside them. Badgers are clean animals and dig small holes

▼ Badger's sett with pile of earth outside.

TIP • TIP

• Carry a plastic bag in your pocket on a walk if you want to collect small items of interest. Then you can keep your pocket and hands clean.

Links

making jewellery p.113

to serve as their toilets a little way from their setts. If there is a sweet musty smell around the entrance, that's more likely to be from a fox.

If the hole has cobwebs covering it, then it is probably not in use. Look for fresh paw prints in the entrance holes and scraps of dry grass bedding along the runways.

You can find out if an entrance is being used by laying two light twigs across the mouth of the hole, so that an animal can't get past without moving them. Then come back the next day and see if the sticks have been brushed aside.

Look out for animal pathways through grass and other long vegetation. Many mammals, like deer, foxes and badgers tend to use the same routes on a regular basis, so gradually a path is worn. If you are not sure whether a path has been made by an animal or not, look to see if it goes under any low branches. If it does, then it is more likely to be an animal path.

And watch out for the places where such a path crosses a hedge or fence; there tends to be an obvious tunnel-like gap at ground level through the vegetation if the path is being used by a small mammal. If it is a deer path there may be no tunnel, since deer often jump over fences. Look for tufts of hair caught on twigs beside the path or at the fence crossing – the colour may help you to make a guess at what animal is using this path. Badger hair is light grey, with a dark patch in the middle, and a little frizzy.

project

◀ Like stars in the night sky – patterns on a crab shell.

make a collection

At home you can make a collection of things that you find on your walks (cones, feathers, stones, tufts of fur, dried leaves) and even do more detailed drawings of them in your diary if you want. You can use small items like shells or dried seedheads for making jewellery (see p.113). You can use feathers to decorate hats or a head-band, as people have done for centuries, including native north Americans, New Guinea tribesmen and British army regiments.

Using your ears

For a sharp wildlife tracker, sound and even smell are very important – as they are to the animals themselves for communicating with each other. Even just the sound of something moving can alert you to its presence. Almost all kinds of animal communicate with sound; even shrimps in the sea emit an almost constant crackling and various species of fish produce clicking noises.

Crickets chirp, many insects buzz, frogs croak, snakes hiss and rattle, woodpeckers drum on trees with their beaks and gorillas thump their chests; all quite simple sounds compared to those produced by the more sophisticated voices of birds and mammals.

Birds

Every species of bird has its own calls and song, though a few remain quiet for much of the time. Their songs vary from the simple deep booms of a bittern to the complex, musical notes of a nightingale. We call it 'singing' though most birdsong sounds like whistling to our ears. Most kinds of bird only sing in the breeding season – spring and summer, but robins sing almost all year round. Calls are usually single sounds, though they are often repeated, sometimes rapidly, particularly when a bird is agitated.

▶ Yellowhammers sing to the rhythm of 'A little bit of bread and no cheese, please'.

Alarm calls

Alarm calls vary from species to species, but are often sharp 'chak's (like smacking your tongue on the back of your teeth) or scratchy rattles. When birds are agitated, they tend to repeat these over and over, almost in irritation.

If you hear alarm calls from a group of birds, they are probably agitated by a predator on the prowl. In a wood it may be a tawny owl (this is the best sign of a tawny owl out in daylight); around gardens it may be a cat – probably sneaking stealthily through bushes.

There may be a sparrowhawk in the area; they are very agile, fast fliers, and cunning too. They often fly very close to the ground, behind a wall or hedge, so you have to be alert to spot them. And small birds are very alert. Most often you hear a few alarm calls from the small birds because you yourself, or some other human, have just come into the scene.

▲ A Chough making an alarm call.

So the trick is, when there's a disturbance among the birds, think what might be causing it. Army scouts are well aware of this and many soldiers owe their lives to sharp ears and an alert mind.

If you want to begin learning bird sounds, start with the songs or calls you hear most frequently in your garden or on a walk to school. Take a look at what bird is making the sound and try to describe in your mind what kind of sound it is, so you can remember it. See if you can learn to recognise the magpie's loud, rattling call.

Nature Safari

Mammals

Foxes bark and shriek, deer bark and bellow, badgers whikker, otters whistle and seals sing. Most mammals have a few calls, but the sounds they make are rarely as complicated as birds. Shrews are quite vocal animals: they chatter in a very high-pitched, squeaky voice that is difficult for older people to hear. Young people can usually hear them with no trouble.

There are some mammals, including bats and dolphins, that have developed a very special sound skill – they use *ultrasound* for hunting.

▲ Foxes call at night, especially in mid-winter.

Both these creatures make very high-pitched clicks – too high-pitched for us to hear. But their hearing is finely-tuned to this pitch and they form a picture in their mind's eye from hearing the echoes of the clicks. A moth flying by or a small fish in the area will change the pattern of the echoes and whoosh – breakfast for the bat or dolphin.

Using your ears

This has one great advantage for the creatures with this ability: they can move and hunt in places with no light as if they had night eyes. So dolphins can hunt in murky waters and bats can hunt at night. What is more, you needn't worry about a bat bumping into you in the dark and getting tangled in your hair (an old story); they can see you with their ears and would definitely prefer to avoid an encounter with such a ugly monster (to a bat, of course!).

On the other hand, some creatures use infrasound – too low for us to hear. Elephants are thought to contact each other over quite large distances using a very low-pitched rumbling.

- Frogs and toads courting in ponds in the early spring. Choose a warm sunny day (not too early) or a mild, calm evening.
- Songbirds dawn chorus: any bright morning from late winter to early summer.
- Nightfall in May in a nightingale wood.
- Visit a woodland on an early spring morning and listen for the drumming of woodpeckers.
- Sea-bird colony: spring and summer. Listen for the laughing cackles of fulmars greeting each other and the almost human purrs and grunts of the guillemots.
- Grasshoppers thrumming away on a warm sunny day – in grassy sand dunes, meadows, heaths and moors.
- Grey seals: the haunting songs of the females can be heard most of the year, but including their basking sites in summer. But try visiting a breeding colony in November – there are several with access to visitors. The pups sound just like human babies – really eerie.

▲ Some woodpeckers make a drum roll sound by rapidly bashing a tree with their beak.

Nature Safari

Tuning in

A good opportunity for hearing some more unusual sounds and tuning in to the wildlife channels of the night and early morning, is to go camping. You can listen for owls, deer and foxes as you go to sleep and the birdsong when you wake up. There is only a thin nylon sheet between you and the sounds around, so you can hear them quite clearly. The only problem is that the birds may wake you very early!

Wild choruses: when and where?

• Large flocks of geese that breed in the Arctic spend the winter in the milder conditions scattered across European lowlands. They have a regular daily routine of moving between daytime feeding grounds and safe night roosts. If you find out where a roost is (the RSPB can help) and get there for the late afternoon in winter, you could hear the magic of the goose tribes – a thousand excited voices passing just overhead. Just a note: whereas farmyard geese and greylags have quite harsh voices, some of the wild geese species have more melodic voices.

▲ When frogs are gathered for breeding they can become very loud.

TIP • TIP

• If you want to listen a bit more clearly to something in the distance, cup your hand around one ear. You can take this principle even further by making a funnel from some paper card (tape the seam down). Leave a small hole at the tight end and put this to your ear. This is excellent for listening to grasshoppers too.

Using technology

Try to find a small magnifying glass that can fit in your pocket; one that folds into an outer case is ideal. This will open up the small-scale world for you – tiny flowers, small insects and spiders (take a look at their faces!). If you want to delve into the minute world, you will need access to a microscope; your school might have one. Depending on its magnifying power, this can reveal mites, plankton in pond water and a whole variety of tiny monsters invisible to the naked eye.

Binoculars

Because wild animals are usually scared of people, they keep at a distance from us, so a pair of binoculars is a great help for getting a better look. Often they are essential if you want to positively identify a creature. They take a little getting used to – practise finding and focusing on particular subjects through them. They are very useful for watching birds and larger mammals like deer, watching the sea for boats or dolphins, and also for looking at the moon. But never, EVER point them at the sun – you will damage your eyes.

Telescopes have even more magnifying power than binoculars. Great, you might think. But as the magnification increases, so does the difficulty of holding a steady image. Telescopes need to be rested on something, ideally a tripod.

▼ Binoculars are also good for sea-watching.

Nature Safari

Photography

Photographing plants and animals can be very rewarding, but it tests your patience. It is like hunting, without harming anything: as well as capturing the beauty of some of the creatures around us, it is also a good way of learning more about your subjects.

Although birds make great subjects, they are very difficult to photograph in the wild. Their wariness and quick reactions mean you often end up with a blurred or even an empty photo: the bird took off just as you pressed the camera's button (see below for some ideas of where to photograph birds). Also the experts use expensive telephoto lenses that magnify distant subjects, so they get a more detailed image filling the photo frame. It is less frustrating to begin with some easier subjects – preferably more approachable and not so quick moving.

You could practise with wild flowers or leaf shapes, though even with these 'still' subjects, you should take your photos in calm conditions – a leaf in the wind makes a blurred photo. As you become more practised try insects – butterflies make good subjects. But here you need to sharpen your stalking skills to approach the insect without frightening it.

Butterflies are most easily photographed when they are resting or sunning themselves; when feeding, they often keep moving, though a close-up photo of a feeding butterfly would be a real prize.

You will need to check a few things about your camera. How close to your subject can you get and still focus on it? Will your lens magnify the subject? Flowers, leaves and particularly insects are small subjects and, to get a good photo, you will need a camera with a lens that can enable you to get a close-up. Ask for advice to help you check this, if necessary.

For the best results, use a tripod. This will help you to keep the camera even more steady; the slightest movement when you take the picture will increase the blurring (smudging of detail) in the photo.

Watch out for very bright patches in your picture (highlights). White and yellow petalled flowers and insects with shiny parts can be difficult to photograph in bright conditions, where the rest of the picture has duller colours. You will need to make some appropriate adjustments, if the highlights are to come out sharp rather than washed-out.

▲ Flowers are a good starting point for nature photography

▼ Frogs can keep still for long periods

Frogs and toads are good to photograph, if you approach them carefully, but many animals are just too wary to allow someone close enough to take a photo. Nevertheless, if you think about it there are all sorts of places where you'll have a good chance. Squirrels, birds and maybe deer in a park; swans and ducks if the park has a pond; hawks and owls at a birds of prey centre; gulls in harbours and possibly seals.

If you have access to a computer and a scanner you could scan some of your photos and make your nature diary into a website. You can take patterns or details from your photos and develop illustrative designs. Maybe you could get help through your school if you would like to do this.

While on the computer, if you can access the internet, this is a good place for research about species, habitats or actual places. There are many pages for both beginners and specialists. The websites of the organisations listed later should provide you with some good links to get started.

project

map reading

There are two great reasons for learning to read maps: firstly, it helps you find your way about; and secondly, it enables you to discover some interesting places. Under the first comes 'not getting lost'. It may take you some time to learn to read a *compass* properly, but basic map reading skills are not difficult. Map reading is a good ranger skill and a good survival skill.

Step 1: Get a large scale (e.g. 2cm to 1km) Ordnance Survey map of where you live.

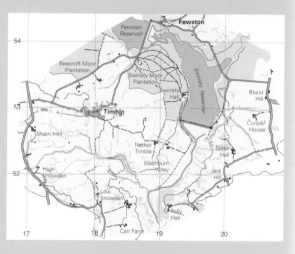

Step 2: Check what the most common symbols mean in the key down the side.

Step 3: Find your home on the map.

Step 4: Line up your map on the floor, with the top to the north, by comparing the map with the streets around your home.

Now you have a basic plan for reading any place. Try drawing your own map of an area – your garden or the streets around your home – and mark on it symbols for the things that interest you.

Links

find an iron-age or Roman fort p.23

Our environment:

conditions on planet earth

A NASA Earth Observatory image

The atmosphere and its weather

The climate in northern Europe

The earth goes through occasional colder spells. A mere 15,000 years ago, northern Europe was frozen and much of it was covered with ice. 15,000 years may sound like a long time, but it is just a passing scene in life's constant evolution. Not much grew, so there were few animals and our ancestors were not able to live in these conditions.

But as the world warmed up again, and summers passed, trees returned to colonise the open spaces. Weeds, grasses and shrubs grew first, then the big, slow-growing forest trees. High forest is the natural habitat for most of our region, where the ground isn't too wet, too steep or too high.

Some scientists think that a cold period, caused by a meteor hitting the earth around 65 million years ago and raising a huge dustcloud that blotted out the sun, was the reason the dinosaurs became extinct. They were cold-blooded animals, that need the sun to warm their bodies up, and just not able to adapt to the colder conditions.

Why the weather changes

Sunshine, wind and rain: temperature, exposure and moisture. These are the main ingredients of the weather mix. But let us step back a moment and see what's happening on a larger scale. The earth is a giant tennis ball suspended in space: each day it spins one whole revolution, causing night and day, and each year it rocks back and forth gently on its axis (from north pole to south pole), causing the seasons.

It would be a dark, frozen world, but for a gigantic beach ball of a sun, blazing bright and radiating heat 150 million km from our earth. (It takes light 8.5 minutes to reach the earth from the sun.) Get your deck chair out and while sunbathing consider this: the earth is not all heated up equally. The part of the earth that is pointing towards the sun gets the most heat. But this is always moving as the earth spins and rocks.

The crusty surface of the earth is literally dripping in moisture – so much so that massive, no – GARGANTUAN – puddles have formed covering a full two-thirds of the surface. These are the seas and oceans.

Wrapped around the surface of this world is a thin layer (several kilometres thick, in fact, but on the scale of the tennis ball, less than a millimetre) of mixed gases – the Earth's atmosphere. When we breathe, we

▼ Weapon of Zeus or raw electrical energy?

Nature Safari

take in the air's mixed gases and our lungs absorb some of the oxygen. All animals need oxygen. Oxygen makes up about a fifth of the air, nitrogen about four fifths and there are small amounts of other gases.

Differences in heat make the gases in the atmosphere drift and swirl, as hot air rises and water evaporates to form clouds. The result is our changing weather. Sometimes it is clear and the sun shines down; sometimes the sky is thick with clouds, blocking the sun's warmth.

Spirits in the sky

Many peoples have worshipped the sun as the source of all life. The ancient Egyptians believed that the Pharaoh was the son of Re, the sun god and the most important god in their religion. The Japanese used to think the same of their Emperor. Now we say the sun is the centre of our solar system – solar means 'of a sun'.

And from the great Hall of Lightning comes the Norwegian god Thor, riding his chariot through the sky and brewing storms by blowing through his beard. Thunder was his tool, just like the thunderbolt was thought to be Zeus' weapon by the ancient Greeks. When Zeus was angry, the sky rumbled and, when his rage broke, lightning flashed. Well, it was the best explanation for thunder and lightning at the time.

Thunder

When you see the flash, count how many seconds until you hear the thunder. This will tell you how far away the storm is from you. There are about 3 seconds for every kilometre between you and the lightning bolt. Why is this? Because light moves so fast it is almost instantaneous; but sound travels much more slowly, at around 800km per hour. (And for the record, light travels at about 300,000km PER SECOND – as fast as you can see!)

Thunderstorms usually happen in warm, humid conditions. They are caused by the build up of an electrical charge in the moist clouds. When it reaches a critical point, it discharges the electricity to earth in a massive spark. It takes the shortest path to earth, so tends to strike tall trees, church spires and other tall buildings. That's why it is dangerous to shelter under a tall tree in a thunderstorm, but very few people have ever been hit directly by lightning.

Weather forecasting

I remember an old man saying to me when I was young: 'When you can read the clouds, you'll be a wise man'. It didn't make much sense to me then, but the saying stuck in my mind. And now I'm beginning to think it's true.

It is a great skill to understand weather conditions and be able to predict changes. Cloud formations are good indicators, since the changing patterns are caused by variations in the local conditions of the earth's atmosphere.

▲ Evening clouds make beautiful patterns.

The main types of cloud formation

Cirrus (curl of hair) – *wispy or streaky, high up, tiny ice crystals: strong winds. Unsettled weather.*
Stratus (layer) – *in layers, lower. Dull, could be wet.*
Cumulus (heap) – *fluffy, low to mid-height. Fine, but possibility of showers later.*
Cumulonimbus – *towering piles of cloud. Thunder and lightning (and tornadoes).*
Fog – *clouds at ground level. Very quiet.*

Before we had weather forecasts by the professionals on TV and in newspapers, people used to look for signs that might indicate approaching weather patterns. They were particularly interested in any changes in the behaviour of animals and plants: such things as ants moving to higher ground, spiders coming into the house or sheep's wool uncurling in low air pressure, which usually brings poor weather.

▼ Pine cones open in dry weather.

But many plant and animal weather signs are based on their reactions to the weather as it's changing; you do not get much advance warning. Pine cones open in dry weather and shut in wet weather, so once you see the sign, the weather will usually have changed already!

There's an old saying you may have heard: 'Red sky at night – shepherds' delight. Red sky in the morning – shepherds take warning.' Why not find out how often this is true. Make a note in your diary when there is a red sky in the morning or evening; then make a note of what the weather is like on the day (the day following the evening red sky and later the same day as the morning red sky). Autumn, spring or winter would be the best times to check this, since in summer sunset is late and dawn is very early.

▲ Snow forming a cold, white blanket on the earth.

Rain and snow

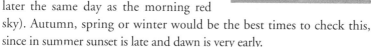

Rain falls when water moisture in the air (evaporated from the seas) gathers and cools. The amount of rain that falls varies from place to place: deserts get very little rain at all. Europe varies from dry, arid semi-deserts in the south with just occasional rain, to wet coastal mountains of the north and west with over 1m of rain per year. Rainfall is usually measured in terms of the amount that falls in a year, to allow for monthly differences. When the temperature falls to around freezing point (0°C) and below, rain falls as snow – frozen water crystals.

▼ Frost and snow sculpted by the wind can produce some unusual shapes.

Morning dew is not produced by an overnight shower, but by moisture in the air condensing on vegetation in the cool of night.

Fresh water is essential for all life. But too much rain falling at once can cause floods and be very destructive. And rain in cold conditions can make life hard for some animals.

project

make a simple rain gauge

Get an empty plastic bottle and ask an adult to cut off the top part, where it narrows to the opening. Then turn the top part upside down and tape it inside the top of the rest of the bottle, so that it is acting as a funnel. Mark measurements from the bottom of the bottle in centimetres on the side. This will do to measure longer showers of rain; it won't be accurate enough for light rain showers.

Wind

Many ancient peoples believed that winds contained spirits. It is easy to see why: it sometimes feels like winds are alive. They roar and rustle in trees; they whip up dry leaves into spirals and ripple the surface of water; they can hit you in sudden surprise gusts, as if chasing you down. In Greek myths the god Aeolus kept the winds in a sack and depending on his mood he would let one or other out to blow. They had names: Boreas was the north wind.

A more scientific explanation is that wind is movement of the air, produced by variations in the heat of the earth's surface. As hot air rises, cooler air is sucked in to replace it. On a hot day in coastal regions, cool breezes from the sea often develop, since the land heats up more quickly than the sea.

Wind-chill

In winter and on cold days when the wind is blowing, choose a sheltered place for a walk. The stronger a wind blows, the more heat we lose from our bodies and the colder we feel. Calm, frosty days make for better outdoor days in winter than cool windy days.

The Beaufort Scale
(named after Admiral Beaufort who invented it)

Force	Wind	km/h	Signs
0	Calm	0–1	Smoke rises vertically
1	Light air	1–5	Smoke drifts slightly
2	Light breeze	6–11	Feel it on your face: leaves rustle
3	Gentle breeze	12–19	Twigs move; light flag unfurls
4	Moderate breeze	20–29	Dust and paper blown about; small branches move
5	Fresh breeze	30–39	Wavelets on inland water; small trees move
6	Strong breeze	40–50	Large branches sway; umbrellas turn inside-out
7	Near gale	51–61	Whole trees sway; difficult to walk against wind
8	Gale	62–74	Twigs break off trees; walking very hard
9	Strong gale	75–87	Chimney pots, roof tiles and branches blown down
10	Storm	88–101	Trees uprooted; severe damage to buildings
11	Violent storm	102–117	Widespread damage to buildings
12	Hurricane	Over 119	Devastation

A traditional way of telling from which direction the wind is blowing (if it's not obvious), is to lick one side of your finger and hold it up to the air. Whichever direction feels colder on the damp skin is facing the wind. I find it easier to pick up some dry leaves or grasses and toss them in the air; the wind carries them a little way in the direction it is blowing.

Go fly a kite

A good kite flying place has plenty of space and is exposed to the wind. It should be clear of trees and keep well away from any wires, telegraph poles or pylons; in fact if there are any nearby, find somewhere else. The beach or the brow or spur of a hill are good places.

A moderate breeze is the best wind for kite flying. If it is too calm, you will struggle to get the kite airborne; if it is blowing too hard, you will struggle to keep it under control. Run with the kite on a very short string, to get it started, gradually giving it more string as it gains height.

TIP • TIP

• When making a den, or putting up a tent, check which direction the wind is blowing from. Then arrange the shelter so that the entrance or doorway is facing away from the wind.

Raptor watching

Now that you've got a feel for gliding and wind power, why not see how birds use the wind. Large birds of prey like a breeze since this enables them to fly easily, without putting their energy into flapping their wings. In the early spring pairs of many species soar high on bright, breezy days to show that their *territory* is occupied. This is one of the best times to watch buzzards, eagles and, of course, kites – yes, there are birds called kites and they're superb gliders.

Other good gliders are seabirds of the albatross, shearwater and gull families. A bird that is common in some coasts in northern Europe is the fulmar, a small member of the albatross family. You can see them hanging in the breezes that skirt sea cliffs; sometimes they swoop past in fast glides.

▲ Red kite - one of the most elegant fliers.

▼ Fulmars make flying look easy.

Hurricanes and tornadoes

These tropical storms are the result of moist air being overheated. Tornadoes are a kind of jet version of a hurricane. To see how they move, watch a small eddy or whirlpool in a stream. Or watch how bathwater begins spinning as it goes down the plug hole.

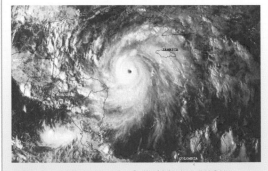

▲ Hurricane Mitch, over the Gulf of Mexico. (NASA)

Nature Safari

project

make a windmill

You will need:
2 beads
Card (20cm x 20cm)
Crayons/paints
Pin
Scissors
Stick (30cm)
Wire (20cm)

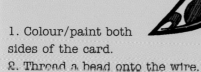

1. Colour/paint both
sides of the card.
2. Thread a bead onto the wire.
Bend the end of the wire so the
bead doesn't come off.
3. Fold the card diagonally (corner to corner)
both ways and open out.
4. Cut along the folds to about 1cm from the centre.
5. Make a hole with the pin in the right side of each corner.
6. Bend each corner into the middle – do not fold,
but hold them together.
7. Thread the wire through the 4 holes,
then through the other bead.
8. Wind the rest of the wire around the stick.
9. Hold your windmill into the wind, or blow
hard on it to make it spin.

The seasons: spring, summer, autumn, winter

The band of the earth in which Europe lies is known as temperate: it falls between the extremes of the hot tropics and the cold arctic. In temperate lands the weather varies according to the season, summers are warm and good for the growth of plants, but the cold winters, with shorter days, don't allow much growth and create more difficult conditions for animals. So in these regions of the world, the animals and plants you might find in any one place varies through the seasons. For instance, in winter the moors can be a barren place and look empty of living things, where on a summer's day they can be full of life; and there are very few plants in flower at mid-winter.

▶ The earth moves around the sun on a yearly cycle and with a tilted axis.

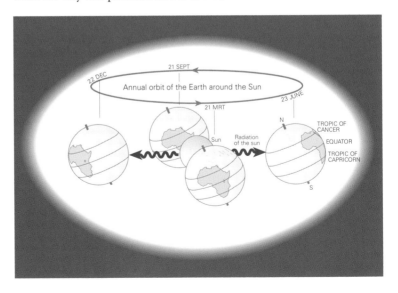

People generally find temperate climates the most pleasant for life. Almost half the world's population lives in the planet's temperate zones, yet they cover only about seven per cent of the land surface.

▲ Changes through the four seasons.

At the Earth's poles, the Arctic and the Antarctic, the seasons are more extreme. In winter, the sun doesn't rise and they are frozen, dark places; in summer, the sun doesn't set, though it rarely gets warm. See if you can find out more about 'the land of the midnight sun'.

Plants and animals cope with the changing seasons in a whole variety of ways: though some species thrive in cool conditions, all living things struggle to survive harsh winter weather. The fur of many mammals grows thicker in the autumn to keep them warm; some hibernate through the coldest months. Many birds migrate further south for the winter and return the next spring (usually to the same place as the previous year). The leaves and flowers of most plants die back and just the roots or stems survive to produce green shoots when the sun grows stronger. Insects mostly hibernate or spend the winter as eggs from which a new generation hatches the next year.

The seasons: spring, summer, autumn, winter

Signs of the changing seasons

Spring
- birds singing and building nests
- geese flying north
- frog & toad spawn
- blossom on trees
- lambs in fields
- hares boxing
- leaves sprouting on tree branches
- days get longer
- the sun higher in the sky

Summer
- birds with young
- flies on the wing
- butterflies and dragonflies
- long grass and flowers
- trees covered in leaves
- the longest day
- green trees

Autumn
- birds flocking
- swallows gathering on wires
- fruit and nuts on trees and bushes
- days get shorter
- wasps coming into the house
- leaves changing colour and falling
- geese flying south
- dampness
- mushrooms and fungi in woods
- salmon jumping waterfalls

Winter
- frosts and ice
- bare trees
- brown grasses and dead leaves
- short days
- sun low in the sky
- few insects about
- rusty coloured bracken
- birds and other animals fluffed out against the cold

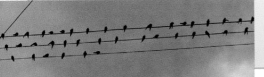

Charting the seasons

▲ Swallows gathering for their long journey to Africa.

Why not enter your own observations in your diary? Note down all the things you see reminding you that the season is changing. Or you could pick one thing and note how it changes from day to day or week to week. You could make a note of each new flower you see from the end of winter onwards (different plants produce their flowers at different times). Or you could keep a note of when you first see different kinds of insects from late winter onwards.

If you put a thermometer outside your house, you can record the temperature each day (ideally at the same time each day). Hang it about 1.5m from the ground, in shade on an unheated wall (i.e. not by your boiler outlet or on a chimney). If you can, get a thermometer that measures minimum and maximum temperatures. You may get a surprise at the overnight frosts. This is a project you could do with your school. You can also measure rainfall quite easily by collecting it in a jar. You need an anemometer to measure wind speed, but you can get a rough idea from the indicators on the Beaufort scale (see p.169).

Links

for making a rain gauge, see 'rain and snow' p.168

Nature Safari

When birds sing

There is a lot of interest in the date of different birds beginning to sing in the spring. Blackbirds are an excellent indicator of warmer weather: they are common, easily recognised (well the males are – they're totally black with an orange beak and eye-ring) and have a fairly distinctive and very tuneful song.

▼ Male blackbirds begin to sing towards the end of winter.

Keep an ear out from Christmas on, for when your local bird starts to sing. Mornings and evenings, even in the twilight, are best. In the south they should be singing in any mild weather from Christmas onwards; in the north and in hill country it could be April before you hear much if there is bad weather in March.

Recently, people have commented that birds seem to be singing earlier in the year than they used to. Now scientists have begun investigating whether this is true, since it could be a sign that the earth is getting hotter ('global warming').

TIP • TIP • TIP • TIP • TIP • TIP • TIP • TIP • TIP
Seasonal behaviour

• It is possible to see anything, provided it lives in your area and you do a little research; but since so many animals' and plants' lives go through yearly cycles, it is no good looking in the wrong season. Let's say you want to see that rare lizard in the wild, the one you saw a snippet about on the TV, that's supposed to be somewhere in your area. You need to know what kind of habitat it is found in, and what its seasonal habits are.

• You may have to plan up to a year in advance – but that only makes it more special. Be patient and look forward to the encounter with pleasure. Maybe you could find out a little bit more about the species: why is it rare? Many rare species are specialists who no longer find many places suitable for their needs. So what makes it different?

Links

changing seasons, project – keep a diary p. 16

The sky

Day and night

The earth spins on its axis, like a top, turning one full revolution every twenty-four hours. We know the full circle better as a day and a night. It's night-time for the half of the earth facing away from the sun.

Although it is the spinning of the earth that causes night and day, it appears to us that it is the sun that's moving, rising in the east and crossing the sky to sink down in the evening in the west. The Greeks thought the sun was the shining chariot of the sun-god being driven across the sky. In fact they believed all the heavenly bodies – the planets, our moon and stars were gods, goddesses and legendary heroes.

▼ Daylight for half the world – night for the other half.

NASA

All the same stars are up in the sky during the daytime too, but we can't see them. The light from our sun is so bright that the tiny light from distant stars is just unnoticeable.

It is mind-boggling to think that all the little dots of light in the night sky are actually other worlds, many of them much larger than our planet earth. Most of them are distant suns and among them the other planets of our solar system and our moon. Though we cannot see them without special telescopes, each of the distant suns has its own system of planets and their moons; and in the space between these larger bodies there are comets and asteroids. This is our universe – whole *galaxies* of stars stretching out in all directions into space for as far as you can imagine.

Not quite to infinity though. The brilliant Albert Einstein worked out that space is curved, so if you head off in a straight line for ever and ever, you will eventually come back to the place you started. Einstein's theories are not easy to understand, but scientists believe he provided the best explanation for the laws of the universe.

Watching the stars

The air is often clearer in autumn and winter for viewing the night sky, and it helps if you keep away from streetlights and any other sources of electric light. If you want to see the starry night at its best, also pick a night with no moon. Then you should be able to see a dark sky filled with thousands of tiny stars. The pale band across the middle is an area that is densely packed with stars known as the Milky Way – this is our *galaxy*.

Among all the stars are several lights which don't twinkle so much: these are the other planets in our solar system. The stars are actually suns like ours with their own planetary systems around them. The planet Venus is the easiest to recognise since it is the brightest and nearest planet to earth; it is best seen around dawn and sunset and has been called both the Morning Star and the Evening Star.

People who study the stars are called astronomers. So far no sign of life has been found anywhere else except earth, but many scientists believe there probably is other life out there on some planet in a distant solar system.

Planets in our system

- The sun: the centre and source of all energy.
- Mercury: no atmosphere.
- Venus: surrounded by clouds of poisonous gases.
- Earth: the blue planet – home to all known life in the universe. One moon.
- Mars: the red planet, because of the rusty dust from iron. Cold, no air, dust storms.
- Jupiter: gigantic. Mostly gas and liquid. Monstrous storms (e.g. a 300-year-old storm). Sixteen moons.
- Saturn: large. Mainly gas and liquid. Rings made of rock and ice fragments. Lots of moons.
- Uranus: very cold. Mostly gas and liquid. System of rings. Fifteen moons.
- Neptune: very cold. Mostly gas and liquid. System of rings, just visible.
- Pluto: tiny (smaller than Earth's Moon). One moon. Very cold and dark. So far away that we cannot see much of it even through the most powerful telescopes.

NASA

Gravity

All bodies of solid matter have a force that attracts other matter, rather like a magnet. This is called gravity and it is the force that keeps the planets and other bodies in our solar system in balance, moving along regular paths. It is the earth's gravity that keeps our feet on the ground and stops us floating off. The gravity of the moon is less strong and you would be able to jump six times as high.

The moon

The closest solid body to the earth is our moon. One night, when the moon is big and bright, take a look at it through binoculars or a telescope. You will see the land shapes of the moon; you should be able to see the circular marks of craters, formed when pieces of rock flying through space have crashed into it.

It appears that the moon changes shape, growing then gradually disappearing each month (29.5 days if you want to be strictly accurate). This is the time it takes for the moon to travel on its path around the earth; the amount of the moon that the sun shines on varies along this path and we only see the sunlit part. The gravity of the moon has one major effect on the earth. It pulls at the world's oceans and seas and causes the rise and fall of the tides.

▼ Constellations – seeing shapes in groups of stars.

URSA MINOR

Polaris

Pherkad
The Guards
Kochab

Dubhe
The Plough
The Pointers
Merak

URSA MAJOR

Groups of stars have always suggested shapes to people and this helps to remember their positions. One of the best known *constellations* is the Great Bear, though it is also called the Plough and the Saucepan – rectangular with a bend in the handle. Sailors in the past have used the stars to find their direction at night; amazingly, so do birds on migration.

Sometimes, on a crisp, clear night, you may be lucky enough to witness the Aurora Borealis or northern lights. This is when various coloured lights form moving patterns across the night sky, caused by particles from the sun hitting ice crystals in the earth's atmosphere.

Nature Safari

Rainbows

It used to be said that you would find a pot of gold at the end of the rainbow. Once you know how a rainbow works, you realise you can never get to the end. True, you can pinpoint where a rainbow ends, but once you get there, either the rainbow will have disappeared or it will appear further off. What you see is the effect of sunlight hitting raindrops in the distance. Maybe it brings luck with a brighter outlook, like sunshine after the rain.

▲ Sunlight on raindrops – a rainbow.

A rainbow is made up of seven primary colours and these are sometimes called the 'colour spectrum'. In fact, white light is a mix of these colours. In certain conditions light gets split into its basic colours when it passes through glass or water.

You can set up this same spectrum with a light source and a lens, preferably a prism. The lens splits the light into different colours as it passes through. If you do not have a lens or a prism, try a glass of water. Get a tall glass filled with water and hold it up to the window when the sun is shining through. The sun should produce a mark with all the rainbow colours on the window sill as it shines through the glass.

It is true that you only see a rainbow with the sun behind you.

Dawn and sunset are also good times to look at the sky; sometimes there can be spectacular lighting effects as sun paints the changing cloud shapes in glowing red and purple colours.

TIP • TIP • TIP • TIP • TIP • TIP • TIP • TIP • TIP

How to remember the colours of a rainbow

Richard Of York Gave Battle In Vain.

Take the first letter of each word and you have the first letter of the rainbow's colours: red, orange, yellow, green, blue, indigo, violet.

Solid ground

What's the earth made of? Well, it is hard to believe, but the inside of the earth is a mass of red-hot rock, like you see in lava flows from a volcano. In fact volcanoes are like blow holes that let out the molten rock when pressure builds too high. Towards the centre of the earth it gets even hotter and is largely composed of liquid metals.

The surface of our planet, the land on which we walk and the sea bed, is a hard crust, several miles thick, on the surface of more *fluid* rock beneath. But now consider this: gradually over *aeons* of time parts of the crust move about, so the earth's continents as we see them today were not always like this. In fact, at one time South America was part of Africa: if you look at an atlas, you can see how it fits in, like pieces of a jigsaw.

The land of Britain and Ireland comes from two completely different sources. Whereas the southern half was part of the European continent, northern Scotland was part of the same land mass as Greenland. Then it split away, well before even the age of the dinosaurs, and drifted into the edge of the European crust.

▼ Notice the lines in the rock, showing how the ground has shifted over millions of years.

These are the sort of ideas that geologists deal with: they study the nature of rocks. By looking in detail at differences in layers of rock, they can work out the long-term history of a piece of land; they can predict where to drill for oil or where to dig for metals.

Nature Safari

Igneous – Metamorphic – Sedimentary

There are several types of rock which differ in their make-up or composition: igneous, metamorphic and sedimentary. Igneous means 'from fire' and these rocks have been through a molten stage and become fused by heat. Metamorphic rocks are those that have changed through intense pressure and heat. Sedimentary rock is produced when sands and muds (which are particles of other rocks and organic material eroded by the weather) solidify over time into rock.

▲ Fossils – the imprint of prehistoric life.

Fossils are found in sedimentary rocks; any trace of the object that might leave a fossilised imprint disappears when the rock goes through a molten stage. Sedimentary rocks tend to be younger than igneous and metamorphic ones; that is to say they were formed more recently.

Kinds of rock

Granite, marble, limestone, sandstone, coal, slate, diamond. What is the difference between a lump of coal, pencil lead and a diamond? Very little. They are all formed of the same basic substance, carbon. But they have a different microscopic structure. And, of course, you would be daft to pay the same price for coal as for a diamond.

Minerals

There are many different types of rock and they are all made up of different minerals. Minerals are mixtures of chemicals that occur naturally in the world. Often if you look closely at a rock, you can see that it is a mix of different parts. Minerals sometimes form crystals and some are the product of plants and animals from millions of years ago. Amber is formed from the resin of trees that has hardened over vast periods of time. Sometimes pieces of amber are found with an insect trapped inside – dead, of course, no animal can survive for millions of years even if it did have air to breathe.

Sand is a mixture of small grains of rock, sometimes with fragments of shells in amongst it. Soil is made up of sandy grains, decomposing vegetable matter and moisture.

Precious stones: jewels, gems and crystals

Diamond (clear crystal), emerald (brilliant green), sapphire (mostly blue), ruby (mostly red), topaz (many colours – smoky-yellow rarest), amethyst (purple), pearl (read on).

A raw gemstone, as you find it embedded in rock, is usually rather dull looking. It takes the work of a lapidary ('stone-worker'), with precision cutting and careful polishing, to turn the gemstone into a jewel with sparkle.

▼ Gemstones – we all hope to find one some day.

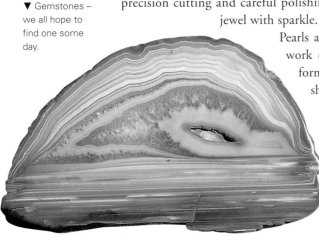

Pearls are rather different. They are the work of oysters – a shellfish. Oysters form the inside of their protective shells with a shiny *iridescent* substance called 'mother of pearl'. When a piece of grit becomes lodged within the oyster shell, this also develops a coating of mother of pearl and so grows into a pearl as we know it. Only a small proportion of oysters have pearls inside them.

Nature Safari

project

grow your own crystals

Crystals grow when a mineral forms layers on its surface.

You will need:
Salt
Jam jar
Pencil
Piece of wool
Warm water

1. Dissolve as much salt as you can in a jar of warm water. Keep stirring and add more salt until no more will dissolve.
2. Tie the wool around the pencil and rest the pencil over the jar, so the wool dangles in the salty water. Leave it in a cool place.
3. As the water cools, gradually the salt will form crystals on the wool.
4. Each day, replace the water with more freshly dissolved salt water.
5. See the crystals on the string get bigger and bigger!
You could continue this project through your school and try growing beautiful blue copper sulphate crystals.

Fool's gold

Gold has always been very valuable to us humans – it is rare and very beautiful. It is found in small seams mixed with other rock under the ground and sometimes in small grains among the gravel of streams. Often when gold has been discovered in an area, miners rush to the area ('goldrush') and are almost driven by a fever – the desire to strike it rich by grabbing a piece of land on which they might find some gold.

BUT … many have celebrated too soon when they have come across rocks with traces of a shiny metal in them. Iron pyrites can look just like gold but is much more common and of very little value. In time it has come to be known as 'fool's gold'. Just imagine if you thought you had the winning ticket for the lottery (let's say 69696); then the next day it was pointed out that your ticket was 96969.

Panning for gold

▲ Gold – would it be so valuable if it was a common metal?

Gold can still be found in some streams of northern Europe, usually in very small quantities of flakes, though occasionally a nugget is found. If you want to be a prospector, use a round pan or bowl (maybe an old frying pan) to sift through sand and gravel scooped from a stream bed. Shake a scoop gently to and fro, letting out the lighter stones that top the pile until you are left with just a little heavier stuff that sinks to the bottom. Since gold is a heavy substance, any gold in the scoop should be there. That's the idea; though you'll need to be very lucky and do some geology to work out where there are likely places; but it is possible to find some.

project

going underground

Step 1: find out where there is a good cave near you that is open to the public.
Step 2: check the opening times!
Step 3: persuade an adult to accompany you there. If you need an excuse, say that a visit to this cave is essential for bringing to life your dull geography lessons.

It is as simple as that. Caves tend to be damp places – they are usually carved out by water. Check out the echoey sounds of dripping water in those dark caverns. See the rock icicles hanging from the roof – stalactites; and those growing from the floor – stalagmites. But the real challenge here is to remember which is which! Just the sort of question for quiz shows. (Here's a line to remind you: 'stalactites hold on tight, but stalagmites might reach the roof').

project

find a fossil

Fossils are the imprint of living things from millions of years ago. Creatures with hard parts to their bodies that fell in mud when they died, are the most likely to be fossilised. The mud hardens to rock over a long period of time, but retains the shape of the animal's hard parts in the grain of the rock. That is why it is the skeletons and shells of animals that are most commonly found as fossils, since these are hard materials; though sometimes leaves and even the wood of trees are found.

▲ Skeletons and shells of animals are most commonly found as fossils

The best places to look for fossils are in *sedimentary* rock outcrops, along beaches or on hillsides. Take care not to climb, since the easiest rocks for findings fossils in are slightly crumbly, which makes them dangerous for climbing. Anyway, you shouldn't need to climb, since there should be a scattering of broken rocks at the base of the outcrop.

The rocks on some beaches are rich in fossils, usually of small shellfish, so it is always worth a look. Another good place to try is a disused quarry; but you will need to take an adult with you and get permission from whoever is in charge of the quarry.

Ask an adult about taking a small hammer and maybe, if they'll help you, a blunt chisel. You could use the hammer to break open some of the rocks; you don't need to bash the rocks – good fossil rocks should split open naturally without too much force.

Further information

Special events and visits

Here are some ideas of things you can do that will take a bit more organising. Some are things you can do in your own time, others are occasional events that may need booking in advance. Check your local paper for details of events in your area or contact one of the organisations in the following section.

Fungal foray

Go out and look for mushrooms and toadstools with an expert in the autumn. Usually take place in woodland.

Bat evening

Enthusiasts in many areas hold bat-watch evenings, where anyone can come along and enjoy the help of experts. They often use electronic bat detectors that pick up the bats' hunting signals. Summer.

Deer watch

The Forestry Commission and local wildlife groups hold deer watching sessions in summer, usually early morning or evening. There may also be opportunities for watching badgers and other mammals through the same contacts.

Osprey, red kite, peregrine falcon and black grouse

There are a number of observation hides in the breeding areas of such birds, where people are welcome to watch large birds of prey at the nest. Mainly April to July. There are also hides set up by the Forestry Commission where you can watch the spectacular display of black grouse.

Visit a wetland nature reserve

Most larger reserves have wooden hides in the best spots and often you can get spectacularly close views of waterfowl, flocks of waders and other creatures. These habitats can also be rich in other wildlife.

Visit a seabird colony

You can go by boat to an island colony (where you may be able to walk among the nesting birds) or take a careful walk along a sea-cliff. Either way the spectacle, the arena of sounds (and the smell!) make this a vivid experience. April to August.

Seaside

Local groups often organise rockpooling sessions, beach art and other workshops. Summer.

Visit a museum

See the different shapes of animals and their skeletons. City museums sometimes have large skeletons, such as those of elephants and dinosaurs. You may also be able to look closely at animals you've only seen in the wild at a distance. Places where you can see captive wild animals include zoos, aquaria, sea-life and bird of prey centres.

Getting into rocks

Visit a cave with stalagmites and stalactites or go on a fossil-hunt with an expert. There are some great caves open to the public with atmospheric lighting installed. Any time of year, but wrap up well in winter.

Climb high

Climb a hill to get a bird's eye view of the land. Anytime of year, but wrap up.

Go camping

Find a comfortable, sheltered campsite, that borders onto some wild land to explore. Best if there are some good paths and no roads. Avoid cold, wet and windy weather, unless you are well equipped.

Organisations

A useful first point of contact for any events or local organisations is the countryside or leisure department of your area council. Often they publish a booklet that lists events going on in the area in coming months.

The Wildlife Trusts
The Kiln
Waterside
Mather Road
Newark
Notts NG24 1WT

0870 036 7711
www.wildlifetrusts.org

There are wildlife trusts for several areas of Wales, Scotland and each county in England. Most, if not all, have junior sections and often special events that might be more interesting for younger people. Each manages a number of nature reserves in their area and will be able to advise you on good sites for seeing things. The address above is for the central organisation; you can get a contact for your local area from them. Local groups hold talks and organise guided visits to sites.

Royal Society for the Protection of Birds (RSPB)
The Lodge
Sandy
Bedfordshire SG19 2DL

01767 680551
www.rspb.org.uk

The RSPB has over a million members, including many younger members in The Young Ornithologists club. Although they are focused on birds, their numerous reserves, which include some of the best wildlife sites in Britain, are also good for other creatures, from insects to reptiles.

When a reserve is managed to maintain a habitat in good condition, it benefits far more than just birds. This is the benefit of an ecological approach. And when we humans can enjoy such places without causing too much disturbance, so much the better.

Staff at the RSPB headquarters (the address above) are used to dealing with enquiries and are in touch with many other organisations, so they are another good place for finding out about events or contacts. They also supervise a number of sites around Britain where you can watch rare nesting birds without causing disturbance, including red kites, ospreys and golden eagles.

National Trust Membership Department
PO Box 39
Bromley
Kent
BR1 3XL

Tel.: 0870 458 4000
www.nationaltrust.org.uk

The National Trust has historic monuments and nature reserves, including many fine coastal areas, which it owns and manages. They usually have a programme of local events, guided walks and workshops particularly in the holiday seasons. Contact local headquarters through the membership department or via their website.

Forestry Commission
231 Corstophine Road
Edinburgh
EH12 7AT

Tel.: 0845 367 3787
www.forestry.gov.uk

The Forestry Commission and Forest Enterprise look after many areas of woodland in Britain. They provide numerous woodland and forest walks, visitor centres, events and activities. Most areas have a ranger or conservation officer who can be approached for advice about wildlife.

These organisations also have special projects that they can link in with schools. If there's something that interests you – some kind of animal, gardening, you would like to set up a wildlife area at your school or study the birds there – ask a teacher to contact one of these organisations. Other projects that can be done through your school might be raising butterflies from caterpillars, hatching frog spawn or feeding birds.

There are many more specialist groups of enthusiasts throughout the country, depending on where your interest takes you: badgers, butterflies, dragonflies, grasshoppers and crickets, whales and dolphins, flowering plants, trees all have their groups of enthusiasts. Any of the organisations listed above should be able to put you in touch with such groups.

If you have access to the internet, this is a good way of contacting these and other wildlife and countryside organisations and finding out more about animals in general. There are many websites covering all aspects of the natural world: try doing a search on a topic and find a site that has a good set of links for the subject you are following.

Safety

Sharp tools and implements Only use sharp tools, including knives, if you have an adult to help.

Hygiene Remember to wash your hands after you've been out or have been handling wildlife or water, and always before eating food. If you have any recent cuts on your hands, you shouldn't put them in pond water.

Water Be extra careful near water – no running; and watch out for soft sand, mud and slippery rocks, especially covered with moss or seaweeds. And remember that rain makes lots of surfaces slippery, so no climbing on wet branches.

Climbing Don't climb up rocks or trees without an adult's permission. And don't climb on buildings, especially ruins, at all.

Exploring Don't wander too far without telling an adult where you're going or asking them to accompany you.

Berries, fruit and mushrooms There are some that are good to eat; but there are some that are very poisonous and some fungi you shouldn't even touch. Don't eat anything unless an adult says it is OK.

Plants Loose clothes are best for brushing through stinging nettles and beware of thorns on thistles, brambles, roses, gorse and hawthorn bushes.

Animals There are not many dangerous animals in northern Europe. Midge and mosquito bites can be irritating; bee and wasp stings are painful and can be dangerous to a few people. Adder bites need medical attention. In the sea, watch out for stinging jellyfish and the spines of weaver fish, which hide in the sand in some regions.

Countryside Code

Leave the land as clean as when you came. If you want to make the top grade as a bush-man, tracker, wilderness ranger or scout, then leave no signs of where you've been. No sweet wrappers, no broken branches or over-turned stones, and in some circumstances, not even footprints.

Don't light a fire without an adult present.

Always close gates behind you so that any animals can't escape.

Don't force your way through fences, walls or hedges; if you damage them, animals could escape.

Don't chase animals, they may hurt themselves or could turn and chase after you! Keep your dog on a lead, so that it doesn't chase and frighten animals.

Always walk around the edge of fields, if there is no footpath. If you walk across, you may damage crops – even if the fields look free of crops, there may be something beginning to grow under the surface.

If you are walking on a road at night, wear light-coloured clothes, so that you can be seen easily.

Always walk facing the traffic on your side of the road, so drivers can see you more easily and you can see them.

Don't pull up plants – it is destructive. In some places it's not allowed even to pick flowers.

Take all of your rubbish home with you – never throw it into rivers or ponds.

Try not to make too much noise or shout. Loud noises will disturb any animals and other people.

Glossary

Aeons vast periods of time (pronounced 'ee-ons')

Algae simple green plants that look like green dust or wool (includes the green slime that grows in ponds)

Allergy when someone's body reacts strongly to a particular substance

Amphibian an animal that lives part of its life in water and part on land

Antenna(e) two long hair-like extensions on the heads of insects and others for sensing what is in front

Antlers the branch-like horns of a deer

Aquatic living in or on water

Arachnids group of related animals made up of spiders, scorpions, harvestmen, ticks and mites

Arthropods group of animals with jointed limbs, including insects, arachnids and crustaceans

Biodegradable can be decomposed by nature

Camouflage disguise for blending with surroundings

Carrion the rotting flesh of dead animals

Characteristic distinguishing mark or style

Chrysalis the pupating stage in the life of an insect, when its body changes from larva to adult

Cold-blooded an animal whose body cannot generate its own warmth

Constellations groupings of stars

Convergent evolution when unrelated animals evolve into similar shapes or forms

Crustacean group of related animals with a rigid outer skin, but no backbone

Decompose break down into its basic parts

Dormant sleep-like state, where the body's processes slow down

Echo-location a way of 'seeing' where things are using sound

Ecologist someone who studies how animals and plants live together

Edible can be eaten

Erosion when the weather, water or ice wears things away

Evolution the way living things gradually change over many generations: some variations survive, others don't

Fertile able to produce offspring; ready to grow

Fluid in a liquid state

Galaxy a vast group of stars

Glacier a very slowly-moving river of ice

Habitat the kind of place where an animal or plant lives

Igneous produced by fire

Instinct a natural tendency to behave in a certain way

Invertebrate having no backbone; the group of animals with no backbones

Iridescent shining with many colours

Larva(e) the caterpillar or young stage in the life of an insect or other invertebrate, when it feeds almost constantly
Lepidoptera butterflies and moths

Metamorphosis period in the life of an animal when its body completely changes
Microscopic on a very small scale
Migration when animals travel to live in a different place – often seasonal
Mimicry where the look or sound of something imitates something different
Mineral substances of the earth, not part from living material
Molluscs group of related animals with soft bodies

Nocturnal active at or connected with the night
Nutrients essential food substances

Organism a living thing – animal or plant

Photosynthesis process by which green plants absorb sunlight directly for energy
Plankton tiny plants and animals floating in vast numbers in the waters of seas and lakes
Predator an animal that catches and eats other animals
Pupa the stage of an insect's life at which it goes through a metamorphosis from larva into an adult

Sedimentary produced by material settling to the bottom of liquid
Shoal group of fish swimming together
Species animals or plants that have similar bodies, live in the same way and can breed together
Stream-lined with a smooth, elongated shape for passing through air or water easily
Synchronise keep in time
Synthetic produced by man through combining substances

Temperate moderate, avoiding extremes
Terrestrial of land, as opposed to air or water
Territory area of land used by and often defended by an animal
Thermometer instrument for measuring temperature
Tropical the central and hottest area around the middle of the earth

Ultrasound sound too high-pitched for human hearing

Venom poison of snakes and other animals
Vertebrate with a backbone

Index